BLACK JUSTICE

IN A WHITE WORLD

A

MEMOIR

ALSO BY BRUCE WRIGHT

•

Black Robes White Justice

Poetry

•

From the Shaken Tower

Lincoln Unversity Poets (Edited with langston Hughes)

Repetition

BRUCE WRIGHT

BLACK JUSTICE IN A WHITE WORLD

A MEMOIR

BARRICADE BOOKS

BARRICADE BOOKS, INC. NEW YORK

Published by Barricade Books Inc.
150 Fifth Avenue
New York, NY 10011

Copyright © 1996 Bruce Wright
All Rights Reserved.

Design and page layout by CompuDesign

Printed in the United States of America.

Library of Congress Cataloging-in-Publication Data

Wright, Bruce, 1918-
Black justice in a white world: the Bruce Wright story /
by Bruce Wright.
p. cm.
Includes index.
ISBN 1-56980-076-6 (hardcover)
1. Wright, Bruce, 1918- .
2. Afro-American judges—New York (N.Y.)—Biography.
3. Discrimination in criminal justice administration—
New York (N.Y.) I. Title.
KF373.W67A32 1996
345.73'05'092—dc20
[B]
[347.3055092]
[B]   95-26656
                                                          CIP

THIS BOOK IS FOR MY SONS

Geoff

Keith

Alexis

Bruce C. T.

Patrick

"THE WORLD WE LIVE IN WAS NOT
MEANT FOR US, NOR WE FOR IT. . . ."

—Horace M. Kallen to his philosophy students
at the New School for Social Research,
at the beginning of each lecture.

FOREWORD

During the seventies, and occasionally, in the eighties, a kind of negative notoriety surrounded my name. As a judge, I was castigated by the police, who accused me of releasing desperate criminals on their own recognizance. The theme of the accusations was that the defendants were "free to do it again," even though none had then been convicted of anything. Ordinary citizens were aroused, too, and they delighted in repeating scornfully the nickname of "Turn 'em Loose Bruce," given me by the Patrolman's Benevolent Association.

My life was routinely threatened. I received the most scurrilous letters. One constant writer said, over and over again, that I should "drop dead twice." There were anonymous threats to kill members of my family to see if I would change my ways. The police, of course, are a tightly knit fraternity. They love their mystique of the "blue wall of silence," meaning that no matter the outrages of brutality they sometimes inflict, no police officer will testify against another. While the mystique remains, it is not entirely intact as several scandals of the nineties demonstrate.

During one hostile episode when the tabloid press carried lurid headlines and a photograph of me that resembled a barbaric fugitive on the run, the head of the PBA demanded that I debate him in public. My response was that I never engaged in a pissing contest with a skunk. That was thoughtless and a reflection of my anger that a group that called its ranks "New York's Finest" could not understand that the jobs of the police, a judge, and the district attorney were all different.

In any event, several people thought my life interesting enough to warrant an autobiography. Toni Morrison suggested that I should write about "what makes Bruce Wright Bruce Wright?" Of course, that would have required as a co-author a psychoanalyst, but I toyed with the idea, out of vanity, I suppose. Prentice-Hall asked that I write about racism in the criminal justice system. I did, in fact, do just that and Prentice-Hall refused to publish the manuscript, saying that there was fear that that firm would be sued for libel. Although I had been paid thirteen thousand dollars, there was never any demand that I return the advance.

For a long time, I resisted. I had never mugged or robbed anyone or committed any other felony. I was never a dope addict and had never searched for or wished to find God. I had smoked marijuana and even joined the national organization to legalize that narcotic. I have married five different black women. Three of them have given me five sons. I longed for a daughter and discovered one born to a woman I had dated in 1966. I had a very serious love affair with a white woman whose unusual family invited me to spend a weekend at their Cos Cob estate. A wonderful poet, she begged me to come to the estate, called Crow's Nest. I asked her if it meant Jim Crow. She wept. I felt as though I had a mouthful of ashes. I last saw her in her hospital room where she died shortly thereafter.

My life has been one of episodes, some I regarded as remarkable. During World War II, I met Léopold Sédar Senghor in Paris. He was then a professor in the *Université outre mer* and a world-renowned poet. He liked my poetry and whenever I visited Dakar, after he became president of Senegal, he always had me introduced as a "well-known black American poet." While I was AWOL in Paris after World War II, he gave me a little job with *Présence Africaine*, the publication of French colonial Africans. He fed me, also, introducing me to dinners with courses and the necessity of wine with lunch and dinner. Senghor was and is the quintessential black Frenchman and is now a member of the French Academy, the first nonnative of France to be so honored.

While Senghor described me as his best black American friend, he was always in awe of more famous blacks. He loves Katherine Dunham, and he was deeply impressed when I told him that Ms. Dunham and I once lived in the same West 66th Street tenement. He heaped Senegalese cultural honors upon her. He expressed excessive praise upon me when he learned that, with Langston Hughes, I had edited a volume of work by Lincoln University poets. He also professed to like my first book of poetry, published in England in 1944, while I was a soldier in France. It was Senghor who introduced me to Ralph Ellison, John Oliver Killens, and other black American writers. I've enjoyed the company of James Baldwin, with whom I once drank too much Scotch and ended up on a hospital critical list with a bleeding ulcer. Now and then, in Paris, I would sit with him and Chester Himes, as Ollie Harrington, Himes, and Richard Wright discussed black matters.

In 1946, after I had returned to America, I spent much time in the studio of Romare Bearden and Charles Alston, then in West 125th Street. I loved the smell of paint and marveled at their genius in giving it shape and form. Through my first wife, I met Aaron Douglas, whose murals are at the Harlem branch of the New York Public Library, as well as at Fisk University, where he taught for so many years. Bearden introduced me to Caresse Crosby who, with her husband, Harry, ran the Black Sun Press in Paris. Caresse promised to include my work in a then-new venture, an unusual publication known simply as *Manifesto*. I was flattered, but it was not to be. The Paris of the twenties and thirties was gone forever and those times were not to be repeated. Before any of my poems could be spread upon the pages of *Manifesto*, that wonderful publication, like so many other cultural quarterlies, failed and I never saw Caresse Crosby again after our dinner at what was then Frank's Restaurant in Harlem, with the then-latest edition of *Manifesto* spread magnificently over two tables.

Langston Hughes introduced me to Zora Neale Hurston and to Richard Wright, an almost mythical figure in my mind. Whenever I was in Paris, I never failed to drop in at the Cafe Tournon, where the black expatriates used to gather. Even now, as though in a secret effort to recapture the sense of passion of those times, my Paris hotel is never far from the Tournon near the Luxembourg Gardens.

Theodore Hugh Hernandez gave me a letter of introduction to Gertrude Stein when I told him that I was being shipped overseas in 1943. I carried it with me until after the war. Teddy, as Hernandez was known, ran a classical music appreciation gathering at the Harlem YMCA, and he seemed to know everyone. He obviously assumed that I would survive the great war. In 1946, I was young enough and brazen enough to carry the letter to Ms. Stein's 27 rue de Fleurus address. I was received with surprising and remarkable friendliness and had an opportunity to see the incredible paintings she had there and her library. I felt I was a part of history.

Looking back, I have managed to be on the fringe of places where great people met, without being a confidante of any of them, except Senghor and Hughes. They thought it was worthy of note that in practicing law, I represented many jazz musicians. I have toured the world with Art Blakey and the Jazz Messengers; I have been counsel to John Coltrane, Miles Davis, Horace Silver, Max Roach, Charles Mingus, Benny Golson, Gigi Gryce, John Henry Perry Bradford, Mary-Lou Williams, and the occasional mystic, Sonny Rollins. Traveling with these musicians was an education, and also frightening in some ways, as I watched so many of them kill themselves with one narcotic or another.

While I can say that I committed no felonies, I did go AWOL while in the army after the war in Europe was over. I was the subject of two court-martials while in the forces, both of which are worthy of a description, because it was Alabama's Fort Rucker, and I was lucky.

When I wrote about racism in the criminal justice system, I was wounded and felt deprived when the publisher did not include an index. I also failed to mention any of the many people who aided and abetted that effort. Robert Stewart, then an editor with Prentice-Hall, insisted that I complete the manuscript of *Black Robes, White Justice*, and he worked ever so hard to make it publishable. Nikki Springer provided the comfort of photocopying; Betty Bissram did the kind of research that only an expert could do to authenticate quotations, dates, and places.

This memoir, compiling many episodes in a long life, is a product of endless insistence by Lyle Stuart. He rejected my working title, *Memoirs of an Amnesiac*, and the present title came from Lyle's wife, Carole. I am not a writer. I longed for someone to help me and take down our conversations and disjunctive recollections. Thus, I have tested the patience of Lyle Stuart, and this comes some four years after it was promised. I did not plan it that way, especially at my age, when time is always of the essence.

There are many who nurtured me, one way or another, along the surprising paths my life has taken, not least of whom is Gail Bishop, a secretary, whose life seems to personify the first two syllables of her title, "secret[ary]." With Gail, there is never a wasted word and, indeed, seldom a word.

Marc Jaffe, famous in publishing circles as a first-rate editor, has tolerated my amateurish ways and sought to make this book meaningful. Lyle Stuart, my publisher, who published *Black Robes, White Justice*, when no other publisher would, has also offered me friendship and much generosity. My wife, Patricia Fonville, has given love to me and has shown a remarkable ability to live with and understand whatever my character is or tried to be. She knows all too well why my friends in France define me a *"type,"* or a *"numero."*

PS

I was lucky, also, to have as a friend and mentor, the actor, P. Jay Sidney. Brave beyond reason, a one-man civil rights movement long before it was fashionable, he saw the racism in the theater, on the radio, in film, and on television. He confronted it head-on and paid the terrible price of being fired and placed on a virtual blacklist, as though he was thought to be a part of some Communist conspiracy. I deem it his doing that so many blacks now have roles in television shows. Knowing P. Jay, I suspect he would quarrel with the quality of what is produced, but whether he likes it or not, the black actors and actresses are his babies. He has a wonderful book or books to write, but he's such a perfectionist, he may never write them. That would be a great loss for all of us. He never tolerated fools gladly. He did, however, tolerate me (but not gladly). The only time I try consciously to abandon my immaturity is when I think of him and his angry wisdom.

— BW

New York City, January 1996.

PART I

My father was five feet four inches tall; a
perfectly reasonable height for a pacifist. A survivor of World War I, he
preached to me from childhood the
imagined virtues of imagined peace.

FROM CHILDHOOD

I sat abject, my hands embraced,
knowing not my manner, nor caring more than I knew.
Scarabs seemed to snow about me quietly,
as Scarabs often will. Pale Horse sat upon my lap,
watching Mephisto sharpening his tail;
a broken high C coloratura was trilled
by a pygmy primate grinding a hand-organ.
I drew a deliberate rorschach into the future
and tossed pennies there,
humming with fatherly caution the beloved dissonance
from *L'Histoire du Soldat*.

Oh days of words with no meaning,
humming has ever meant at least a tune;
so, I dreamed of phlyctery in plural
tumbling round-about, and I wondered
    in my quaint lunacy
if meaning ever had gospel for its simple sanctity.

Taught to pray, I spoke to Aunt Catherine's god
and asked forgiveness for a troubled mind
and dismal visions while wide awake.
In such a trance, I sat upon the side of a bier-like bed,

resting upon a sheer linen precipice,
but wool, of course, in winter.
I then spoke with careful civility and
     modest understatement
to a certain pale horse of my waking acquaintance.
We had sat here before, many times. Modestly,
I assumed that our chats were part of his therapy
for him to visit the whole cloth
of my wool-gathered escarpment. He brought a kind
of mute equine effusion, a model to men of
declamatory rhetoric and patriotism. Since my
degree had been won in horse gymnastics, I
was ill-equipped to understand any clue to
the pathological aphasia of Pale Horse.
But the beast (more a noble steed, really), was
always politic and sapient and those
     charming characteristics
were harnessed to a personality that was diffident.
Had he been a mare, he would have seemed demure.
He was always thoughtful when leaving my lap.
He then would sit, eschewing rashness, reflecting
a wise balance all too often alien to men who

thrust their view of history upon time
while wearing designer blinders on their brains.
He was my non-chromatic friend.
Deeply moved by my patience, I assured him that I
would always be a patient. Celibate among
the synergy of stallions, he would eventually
uncross his several legs as with subdued deference,
he hummed a few bars a lachrymose aria from
Verdi's *Requiem*.

PRINCETON

I was born on December 19th, 1918, in the tiny town of Princeton, New Jersey, from which I was not entirely to escape by Underground Railroad until I was fifteen. A town that had a role in the Revolution, Princeton also had a lesser known part of its biography. The picture of Princeton that a first-time visitor receives is one of a tidy little suburban town. On one side of Nassau Street, the main thoroughfare, there are buildings that remind one of an English village; on the other side, there is the carefully arranged university. Built around Nassau Hall, the university's architects could have copied the campus from Oxford or Cambridge postcards. An imposing see-through metal fence protected the university from the suburban peasants whose business was mainly across the street. The students were presumed to be wealthy, and thus were allowed certain excesses not tolerated among the local residents. Whenever university students crossed Nassau Street to the stores, restaurants, and two movie theatres, the students seemed superior, aloof, even insolent. The town's neat and precise divisions were much in evidence during my childhood.

Princeton's acceptance of nonwhites was limited to a Japanese prince, in fact. The university seemed to need a suggestion of royalty to allow ethnic color to mix with its otherwise white-only students. Black sovereignty, however, was not acceptable. African princes had the Princeton Seminary, a laboratory of theological alchemy, where animistic primitivism could be changed to more respectable Christianity. The Seminary, not founded until 1812, was a separate-but-socially-unequal institution, a place for fragile speculation, where faith was allowed to take over when reason failed.

Princeton has a cemetery, a neatly gerrymandered expanse along Witherspoon Street, that extended well down into the black quarter. "Quarter," of course, was too generous a term to describe the town's Negro section. There were gates in that area that were opened on those occasions when segregated Christians of the town—that is, the survivors of the deceased—were allowed their moment of public pomp as they assured the neighbors that they were burying their dead with decently melancholy rituals. There, the dead were separated, even as they had been in life, on the basis of race. There was a Negro section and a white section. My mother and her oldest sister, my aunt Catherine, are buried in the white section. My father lies in the same obscurity he knew in life, in the areas reserved for the black dead.

The society of Princeton prepared its black residents for its final segregation in death by strict separation during life. There was an elementary school on Quarry Street, called the Witherspoon School. It was named for John Witherspoon, an American clergyman born in Scotland and one of the New Jersey signers of the Declaration of Independence.

At the bottom of the town, where the trolley turned west to Trenton, were the two main streets of the black section, Leigh and Birch Avenues. A small grid of streets between Witherspoon and Bayard Lane defined the enclosures within which most black life existed. There were Baptist, Methodist, and Presbyterian churches distributed within shouting distance of each other, although the Presbyterians were not known to exhibit the expressive emotion of shouting. Along John Street, there was an Elks home and across from it was something called the Nemderoloc Club. This spelling of "colored" men in reverse, I came to think, pretty much reflected the ambitions and attitudes of Princeton's black population.

There was no industry in the town. Unions were unheard of. For the whites, the university constituted the town's chief commerce—although there were small businesses along Nassau Street, including two banks and two small motion picture theatres. The blacks who were not employed as waiters at the university eating clubs were generally cooks and maids in white homes. There were several black teachers in the Negro elementary school. There was a black undertaker, but no black doctor.

When I was a child one John Redmon was the director of the Negro YMCA. He startled me once by saying that he slept each night with a loaded pistol beneath his pillow because of his fear of what the local whites might do at any time. That kind of caution and alarm, he said, had been learned in his earlier assignment in Mississippi. He was Princeton's imported black radical.

My character, to a large degree, was shaped by my emotional reactions to the character of Princeton. I have never forgotten events that occurred during my early youth. In some ways, those events have festered, making me always deeply suspicious of white Christians and shocked that blacks should so avidly embrace Christianity. I realized, for example, that the shabby pretension of the local YMCA, with its tawdry amenities, was an institution that jeered at the town's blacks, especially me. For a long time, I had painful reservations about my white mother. I became a closer observer of what I could see of the relationship between her and my father. I began to wonder how the two of them had ever come together, and why I never saw them kiss or embrace, or say the things to each other that I had been led to believe that people in love said. I was not old enough to appreciate that relations between married couples did not exist upon a courting level for all time and that they could take personal liberties with each other that no stranger would dare to take. I began to attribute an almost sinister meaning to whatever I perceived to rest upon some deep-seated racial basis and wicked intent.

MOTHER

My mother was a tall, handsome woman, jolly, and a moderate drinker. She seemed utterly at ease with the black neighbors among whom we always lived. I was nevertheless wary of her obvious enjoyment of the company of Hugh Reading. He was tall, impressive, and obviously of mixed race. He was the opposite of my father in many ways—in stature, in color, and in what I called arrogance. He always seemed military in his erectness. My father, on the other hand, limped from his rheumatic affliction. He was but five-feet-four-inches and always seemed in great distress from his asthmatic attacks. Reading had soft, wavy hair. My father's hair was pretty much like my own; periodically, he would take me to a barber shop and have me completely shorn. It was a Depression haircut and cost thirty-five cents. To this day, every two weeks, I have the very same haircut. I detest the nuisance of combing and brushing. The one time I ran away—or attempted to do so—at age ten, it was Hugh

Reading who was with my mother in my father's car when I was caught. I wanted very much to be like Reading. He often carried a book and had a studious look about him. He looked the way I imagined a professor should look. But I was much more like my father, relatively short and bowlegged with a symmetry that often made me the target of derisive jeers from my playmates.

No matter how baseless my reservations about my mother may have been, they persisted. I was surprised when she gave me a goodbye kiss on the day I was drafted and sent off—first to Fort Dix and later to a dreadful hinterland in rural Alabama called Fort Rucker. She did offer a few words about being careful and controlling my temper about the way things are. She reminded me that at least four of her brothers had served during World War I and all had returned. "So will you," she assured me. It was a straightforward blessing about an unknown future.

ROOSEVELT

The year 1942 was not a happy time to be black in America. I was well aware of the implications of segregation and what it meant in terms of white attitudes toward blacks. I knew, also, that most Negro troops were in labor regiments or quartermaster battalions and that, at that time, there were no combat-ready black units, although some were euphemistically called combat engineer regiments.

A man called Conrad Lynn had, in 1942, sued the United States Government seeking to enjoin it from drafting his brother, asserting, among other things, that racial segregation was unconstitutional and immoral. Quite apart from any technical grounds, it seemed ridiculous to draft American troops to fight against Hitler's brand of racism while America practiced its own. The background and history of that lawsuit cast a terrible shadow over America for me and revealed how the NAACP played a shameful role in the Lynn lawsuit. I will never forget the remark attributed to President Roosevelt when he was told of the litigation. He is quoted as having said, "What's wrong with that: we've always done it that way." Of course, it had always been done that way, and that was the problem, but apparently not to him. I have never understood why the Jews and blacks have venerated Roosevelt as a holy icon. From all of the biographical publications about him, he came across as sharing little of the concern of the time for the plight of the Jews. In terms of any so-called liberal attitude towards Jews and blacks, it was Eleanor Roosevelt who gave some humanitarian gloss to the Roosevelt name. Perhaps Roosevelt shared the same attitudes as many of his generals, including Eisenhower, Mark Clark, and Omar Bradley. But long before my emotional wars with those generals, I knew that Roosevelt, when Secretary of the Navy, had presided over a branch of the military that limited its black personnel to duty as waiters and cooks for white officers. There were no black officers.

SCHOOL DAYS

My first elementary school had only black students. All of the teachers were black, except for music and gym. There was no gymnasium, and the period devoted to gym meant the schoolyard. Irwin Weiss, the gym instructor, was to play a pivotal role in my life when I was ready for college. The other white teacher was a Ms. Garvin. She taught music appreciation. My white playmates, who were neighbors along John Street, went to the all-white elementary school on Nassau Street, or to what was called the Township school, or to the Catholic school, where the few black Catholics of the town also attended. None of the black elders of Princeton seemed to question the segregated arrangement. Indeed, those who might have been expected to object were the beneficiaries of the arrangement, for they were the black teachers. I never knew how they felt about the racial arrangement of the school. No matter how much it troubled me, I was never brave enough to ask.

One of my teachers, Caroline Gates, told me of the blacks who had fought in the Revolutionary War and of the great black intellectuals, some of them fiery, who were making a name for themselves, but of whom I had never heard. There were names such as Hubert Henry Harrison; Alain Locke, the first black Rhodes Scholar; Booker T. Washington, about whom Ms. Gates said she had reservations; and Carter G. Woodson, the historian. Except for Ms. Gates, no other teacher had ever mentioned such names. Learning about them opened wide a new and different world to me, a world in which there were black heroes, black universities, black doctors and lawyers. In the Princeton of my youth, there were no black doctors. It was rumored that a man named

Spaulding was a lawyer, but he was working as a part-time teacher. Black men who had been away to college had returned to work as waiters or in the post office. For a long time, I thought that it was necessary to go to college in order to qualify for such jobs. This was more a comment on my own lack of understanding than anything else.

FAMILY HISTORY

I knew very little about my father's family. He liked to say that he had been born on the tiny Caribbean island of Montserrat and that the only thing to do there was to take water to Antigua and to escape to America. He managed to do that during the heyday of Marcus Garvey. When my father died at the age of fifty-nine, stricken by cancer, his entire estate consisted of one share of Black Star Line stock with a par value of $1 and one copy of *The Negro World*, the official publication of the United Negro Improvement Association that Garvey headed in America. In 1889, when my father was born, Montserrat was a part of the British West Indies. It has remained so, showing no interest in the fever of independence that swept through the Caribbean after World War II.

There have been conflicting stories about the origins of my mother's side of the family and her curious name, "Thigpen." My grandfather was born in 1857, the year of the infamous Dred Scott decision by the United States Supreme Court. The woman he eventually married, a Martin, was born a year earlier. I am told that their parents had come from Ireland around 1825 and settled in Newark, New Jersey. My mother was one of their thirteen children. No remarkable distinction to any member of that clan was ever communicated to me. While many families appear to be able to trace their roots back many generations, that is not the case with me.

In 1928, my father bought a brand new home on John Street. Often, my maternal grandparents lived there with us. While my grandmother seemed fairly placid, I never saw her smile or heard her laugh. Her face was a severe pattern of straight lines. She did say to me once when I was in high school, "You colored people could do a lot more than you do if you didn't talk so much." It was clear that she placed great value on silence, at least for "colored" people.

My grandfather, on the other hand, had a wonderful sense of humor. By trade, he was a cooper. While I did not enjoy his enthusiasm for fishing, I loved his wry comments. He came to my graduation from law school and when I asked him how he enjoyed the traditionally dull speeches, he said, "It was wonderful; I slept through the whole thing."

SCHOOL DAYS II

My elementary school took us through the eighth grade, after which graduates went on to Princeton High School. This was a public school, of course. Some white students, instead of going to the high school, went to The Hun School, or to the Lawrenceville School. These were known as "prep" schools, which prepared graduates for the Ivy League. Negroes, of course, even if they could afford such schools, were not permitted to enter. While I was in the high school, it never occurred to me that Princeton University had a policy excluding blacks. I simply assumed that there were none wealthy enough to attend. The truth about its racial policies would later be brought home to me with the bluntness with which racism was practiced during the thirties.

Ms. Gates had tutored me in all of the subjects she said I would need in high school, except Latin. I suspect now that she had probably attended what was known as a "normal school" to become a teacher and had not studied Latin. She covered algebra and geometry and a great deal of history that was not taught, especially of the kind now known as *black history*. She was my prep school and she never stopped telling me to make certain to enroll in the academic program for those who were college-bound. Naturally, I did as I was told. I often did whatever she suggested. I was in awe of teachers. My father had always urged me to excel, reminding me of his own fourth grade limitations. In retrospect, I marvel that I never heard my mother or father corrupt their grammar by using double negatives.

I would tell my mother of my music appreciation lessons and, now and then, she would buy classical records for me.

One Christmas, after my sister had married, she gave my sister's husband and me a record album of a Rachmaninoff symphony. She said it was a two-record set, and I could have one record and my brother-in-law could have one. She played the piano, apparently, as was said, "by ear." I found it impressive, but believed there was a domestic conspiracy when I was enrolled in music school to study the violin.

I enjoyed high school and felt fortified by what I had learned from Ms. Gates—as she said, to compete with the white students at the school. Many children of university professors were enrolled, reflecting the meager salaries that teachers and instructors received in those days.

I was a member of the school's track team, coached by Irwin Weiss. He was to do what my family and I called a good deed, despite its ultimate failure and the emotional devastation I suffered.

Ms. Gates was not my only influence during my early teens. My mother's oldest sister also lived with us. Aunt Catherine was an enormous woman, who weighed well over two hundred pounds. Behind her back, my brother and sister and I referred to her as fat. She took such an interest in me that she practically adopted me. I spent a great deal of time with her. She had married a Danish seaman named Bensen and she had an apartment in New York where she stayed whenever Bensen was in port. As a special treat, Aunt Catherine sometimes took me with her. Bensen would always cook, and for breakfast, he would make tiny apple pies and hamburgers. It was sublime dining and I felt sorely deprived whenever he had to put to sea, for he was then absent for months.

When I was on the track team, Mr. Weiss insisted that I

could do better than I did. In fact, I always felt that I could beat the number one distance man on the team, but I was embarrassed by my skinny and bowed legs, so I simply followed him during time trials or in races. Weiss threatened to throw me off the team unless I ran up to my potential and stopped trailing the team's ace, Red Hammond. When I finally did run all out in an East Coast invitational meet, I set a school record for the mile run. In addition to the I-told-you-sos of Weiss, he said he was going to discuss a possible scholarship to Princeton. My family was overjoyed. It was 1935, the middle of the Great Depression, and there were no prospects for a college career for me, absent a scholarship award.

I was also on the high school hockey team. Ms. Gates had told me that colored people could do anything that whites do, and often better. I delighted in my membership on the hockey team. We played local private schools and any other team that would play us. George Tindall was our coach and he made plans for our schedule. One day, we were to play against Princeton's freshman team. As we reported to the Hobey Baker Rink, I was stopped at the door and told that no colored could go in. I looked at Coach Tindall. He ignored me and hurried the white team members in. I was simply left there in the cold. I was more furious with Tindall for abandoning me and doing nothing in my behalf than I was at the rink authorities who barred me. I believe that incident was the beginning of a period of absolute detestation of white people. Perhaps detestation is not a strong enough term, for I was filled with fury and hatred. I never thereafter spoke to Coach Tindall, or to my former teammates. At least I could compete in the classroom.

Irwin Weiss knew me better than I imagined. He heard

about my exclusion from the rink. He uttered a curse word he had counseled all of the track team members never to use and promised mysteriously that he was going to work on "something" for me. Before my graduation, I received a written notice from Princeton that I had been awarded a full scholarship. There was great celebration among my family. Aunt Catherine said, "See? I told you you could do anything if you're smart." Ms. Gates wept excited and happy tears. My father began to talk about me becoming a doctor. I would be the first in either branch of the family to attend college. I relished my emotional revenge against Tindall and the hockey team.

THE PRINCETON UNIVERSITY EPISODE

In September 1936, I reported to the campus of Princeton to register. As I stood in line, an upperclassman, wearing an orange armband to advertise his role in offering assistance to new students, approached me and asked my name. I felt nothing sinister in that circumstance and I continued chatting with a fellow freshman from Massachusetts. After a short time, the upperclassman returned and said that the Dean of Admissions wished to see me. While I hated to lose my place in the registration line, I felt nothing was amiss. I was escorted into the presence of Radcliffe Heermance, then the Dean of Admissions. He seemed to tower over me and my bowed legs. He had a rather harsh expression on his face, I thought. He looked down upon me as though I was a disgusting laboratory specimen. He was the first man ever to address me as "mister." "Mr. Wright," he scowled, "Mr. Weiss never told us you were colored when your scholarship was awarded." He then told me that when King George issued the charter of Princeton, there was no provision for racial discrimination, but that there were too many southerners at Princeton, and I would be unhappy at the university and that under no circumstances could I attend.

Despite the warmth of the September day, a polar draft swept over me. Heermance must have seen my distress. Seeking to ease my pain, he only intensified it. In addition to the mention of King George, Heermance decided to give me some of his personal history. He assured me of his friendliness for "your people," adding that he had no objection to colored people. He assured me that his "colored cook" lived under the same roof as his family. Concluding the lesson in discomfiture, he assured me that, during World War I, he had had a colored orderly, whose patriotism was beyond doubt. Nevertheless, he urged me to look about for a college of "your own kind," or perhaps a state university. He could see that I was not comforted by his tale of personal integration. He must have thought that all blacks can find in religion all of the solace they need. He directed the upperclassman to take me to the office of the Dean of the Chapel. Directed to follow the student, I marched behind him like a zombie.

The Dean of the Chapel was Robert Russell Wicks. Frosty in his spectacles, he seemed quite busy, although he

was in his office alone. He stared at me briefly, as he continued adjusting or adding books to a crowded shelf. He began
a soliloquy, the main theme of which was that the race problem
in America—and indeed, the world—was without solution.
He asked me if I was engaged in some kind of trick to embar-
rass the university. He wanted to know if I was like a certain
Communist in the town of Princeton, who was always seeking entrance to places where he was not wanted. He added
that if I was somehow in good faith, I should know that
Princeton had never had a Negro student and was not likely
to. He then indicated that the conference was concluded.
After that confrontation, I have never since trusted white men
with three names.

Moreso, I think, than being turned away from Princeton's
skating rink, my confrontation with Radcliffe Heermance and
Robert Russell Wicks was one of the most destructive
moments in my life. All of the early morning ideals of elementary school lay shattered at my feet. It was then that I
realized suddenly how false were the cheerful assurances
teachers had given that hard study and love of learning, that
fairness and patriotism were characteristics that could help
any of us become president of the United States. I had never
doubted teachers before that awful moment. But on that
September day, there descended upon me the crushing
knowledge that the black children of Princeton had not been
allowed to join the Boy Scouts; that except for the Catholic
church, places of worship of the same God were completely
segregated; that there were unspoken but rigid lines of separation; that there was a white world into which Negroes were
not to trespass; that the white world had fixed a place for
black citizens; and that the beautifully bound copy of the

Constitution that was one of my high school prizes was a false trophy.

As I sat alone, on the campus, waiting for my father and mother to come and claim me, I felt helpless. Perhaps Wicks was right when he said America's problems with race were beyond human solution. That suggested that intervention by some great white bearded presence in the sky had to resolve human divisions. But it occurred to me also that it was the Christian God who had already ordained the separate churches of Christianity's sectarian beliefs among the Catholics, the Protestants, and the even finer distinctions among the Presbyterians, the Methodists, and the Baptists, not to mention the zeal with which each branch of faith celebrated its rituals.

A SUMMER JOB—NOT QUITE

I remember, too, my first summer of work. Ironically, one of my father's white friends, Mike Cremarian, told him of a lifeguard opportunity at a camp in Connecticut, where the camp owner had been disappointed by a high school graduate—leaving the camp in an awkward position, since the law required the presence of a lifeguard when the campers were swimming. Mike recommended me and off I had gone to Camp Moosehead near Canaan, Connecticut. With my qualifying certificate in hand, I reported to Mrs. Jerome, who ran the camp for a select group of wealthy Christian children. It was, as I later learned, just something to do for Mrs. Jerome. Her husband appeared to own a brass works factory in Waterbury.

When I arrived, the camp cook, Filomena Fondevilla, greeted me and called Mrs. Jerome. She came out, smiling, and asked Filomena to summon the new lifeguard. "Here he is," Filomena said, pointing to me. The smile immediately disappeared and Mrs. Jerome seemed to totter. She reminded me of the kind of doddering chatelaine one could find in any number of P. G. Wodehouse books. Almost breathlessly, she said, "There must be some mistake. Colored people cannot swim in the lake. You never should have been sent here. Just a moment." And she disappeared into what was her camp office. Filomena, hearing all of this, said nothing. Neither did I. My racial problems were beginning to descend upon me like a disease. I could hear Mrs. Jerome's voice, but could distinguish no words. From the sound of her voice, however, there was no doubt that she was upset. As I chatted with Filomena, a bible student from the Philippines, he seemed quite content and quite "colored" also, although not as dark as I am. Finally, Mrs. Jerome returned and said that the law required the presence of a lifeguard at the camp and that I could stay until she found a replacement. Apparently, she meant a white replacement, whose skin would qualify him to swim in the camp's lake and rescue anyone in distress. I was shown to quarters above the camp's garage, and given a long pole. I was told that under no circumstances was I to go into the lake, but to stay in a row boat and assist any camper in need by extending to him the pole while remaining in the boat. My qualifying certificate said nothing about such a distant relationship in a rescue operation, and of course I had no intention of altering a rescue so radically.

There was neither a shower nor a bathtub in my garage quarters, so each morning at dawn, I went to the lake, swam, and bathed before joining Filomena for breakfast.

One morning, during my eventful week at the camp, Mrs. Jerome confronted me, accusing me of violating her prohibition against swimming. She seemed to be trembling as she repeated that it was absolutely prohibited for me to swim in the lake. She asked me if I was a Communist, a political allegiance that had never occurred to me, even as it had not occurred to me to join any political party. She asked Filomena to remind me of my restriction to duty with a pole.

Whatever her difficulties were, no replacement arrived by the weekend. That was when Mr. Jerome came to the camp. He arrived in a chauffeur-driven limousine. He was quite a dandy and an almost exact replica of "Esky," the dandified male caricature who used to appear on the cover of *Esquire* magazine. Short and elegant, he was eligible to join the Wodehouse gallery of the uncles of Bertie Wooster. He had a somewhat distant air, as though he only just tolerated his wife's peculiar preoccupation with a boys' camp, where twenty-five select preteenagers were welcomed to wallow in rural luxury. He was called "Jerry" by Mrs. Jerome. She humored him with affectionate flattery. On weekends, one of Mrs. Jerome's sons—then a Princeton sophomore—would also come to the camp. One early evening, I was with Filomena in the kitchen. The Jeromes and the son, Donny Alford, were having dinner. The telephone rang. Filomena asked that I answer it. I told him someone was calling Donny.

He said I should open the door to the dining area and tell him. I said, "Excuse me. Donny, it's for you." I then closed the door. In a second, Mrs. Jerome came rushing into the kitchen, red-faced and angry. She sputtered, "He is Mr. Donny to you!" I told her that was fine, so long as he called me Mr. Brucie. Even more flushed, she went rather unsteadily back into the dining room, as though fleeing from a dread menace.

The next morning, Mrs. Jerome told me that I must leave that weekend. I thought that at least I should go out in style, so I called four good friends and told them to join me at Camp Moosehead for a weekend bash in my garage lodgings. The four arrived in a new Ford and Filomena outdid himself ordering food and sodas. All of us went for a swim in the theretofore all-white lake. We were the happiest campers in Connecticut, before heading back to New York.

Serious thoughts soon arrived, however, for I was without a summer job. My Aunt Catherine worked for some people who summered in East Orleans, a little village midway between Hyannis and Truro on Cape Cod. I was summoned there and given a job as a gardener; that is, I mowed an extensive lawn, weeded flower beds, and each morning at dawn, I went to a nearby lily pond and collected lily pads to decorate the tables of the household. I also presented a shopping list to the local grocer (who was also the postmaster under the same roof) and took the groceries home. It was a delightful job. I received $15 per week, my food, and lodging. I had a large room in a guest house and each Thursday was my day off.

Next door lived Billy Higgins, a ten-year-old with whom I threw a Frisbee and went swimming. It was a wonderful summer. At the end of August, as I was packing, Billy sat on my bed, watching. He was almost tearful and said little. Cape

Cod has many people of Portuguese descent. Some are as brown as I am. Suddenly, Billy, staring straight at me, asked, "Tell me, Bruce, are you Portuguese or a nigger?" Startled and wounded, I simply answered, "Neither." After that, I discouraged further conversation, shook hands with Billy, wished him well, and told him to leave. I wondered, of course, whether he hated the Portuguese or Negroes, or perhaps both. No racial subject had come up in our summer conversations. I've often thought of Billy since those 1936 days. By 1943, he could have been drafted and, for all I know, served in the same infantry division.

Moving from the Cape Cod incident to the one at Princeton made me feel somehow that I was doomed to have such experiences for the remainder of my life. Billy's curiosity about me led me to believe that he had not seen very many Negroes, except for those of us who worked in the saltbox cottages each summer season. Despite his remoteness from any associations with blacks, he had been introduced to the term "nigger." If that little episode did not wholly ruin the summer of 1936, the Princeton experience did, for I had lost an academic year. I did not know it at the time, but I was headed for the loss of another one as well.

BACK TO SCHOOL

A former member of my high school track team, who was a year ahead of me, had gone off to Virginia State College and become a star on its football team. When he heard the story of my academic loss, he said he could get a scholarship for me at Virginia State, based on the fact that I was the state champion in the mile run the year before. I was delighted. So was my father, who had endeared himself to me after the Princeton rejection by saying simply, without a trace of anger, "We'll just have to find another college for him." My mother, clinging to the magic icons of her Roman faith, muttered, "We should have sent him to Notre Dame," as though, during the Depression, it was simply a matter of "sending" a son off to college, despite the absence of resources. The attempt to interest Notre Dame in my rejected soul was a curious adventure, or misadventure.

An application form was sent for and filled out, buttressed by my academic record and letters of support from good old Irwin Weiss who, as he said, knew there was a Jewish quota at Princeton, but never expected that there would be one for Negroes. In looking back at those days, I now realize how naive Weiss was and how calmly he accepted the fact of limiting quotas for Jews. Ms. Gates also supported the application to Notre Dame with a glowing letter, although she had never told me that I could be president.

It was just as well, I thought, when I learned that Virginia State had accepted me. It was a peculiar place and far beyond anything I had ever dreamed of. I had never seen so many beautiful black women, all dressed as though for some special semiformal occasion. No one looked poor. The Great

Depression seemed nonexistent. But I wouldn't forget that, as my Aunt Catherine drove through the entrance gates to the college, we noted an enormous sign stating that it was "Virginia State College for Negroes." The school was just above the wooded hills outside Petersburg, where a black regiment had been slaughtered during the Civil War. Somehow, it hurt to see the words "for Negroes" there, as though the place was bragging about its segregated status.

My scholarship, as it turned out, was a working one. I was assigned to the maintenance and cleaning of the toilets of Williams Hall, a dormitory for male students. I don't remember the name of the senior who supervised me. He was a hulking and menacing-looking football player, who acted as though he passionately desired to live up to his rather daunting appearance. It was a time-consuming job. Apparently, my supervisor, when not playing football, devoted his other hours to inspecting the five floors of Williams Hall and their toilets. I was not a happy laborer. I was cheered when Aunt Catherine assured me one evening on the phone that the application to Notre Dame had been mailed off.

THE NOTRE DAME EPISODE

A slow learner, I assumed that Notre Dame's policies were different from Princeton's Presbyterian bias. Because

Princeton was surprised to discover that I was "colored," it was thought best to advise Notre Dame in advance that I was not white. I was stunned by Notre Dame's response, and the Catholic members of the family seemed ashamed. That response, coupled with the Princeton rejection, was the beginning of my skepticism and ultimate rejection of Christianity. The Christian religion became for me the source of the world's mischief. Notre Dame's registrar, responding to my application, warned me in his opening sentence that "The answer which we must give to your question is no more satisfactory to us than it will be to you." He was certainly right about the last part. The letter continued, heaping dissatisfaction upon dissatisfaction. Elevating majority rule to an article of white faith, the Registrar, one Father Riordan, said that Notre Dame was operated in a way that the university "could accomplish the most good for all concerned." Apparently exhausting his personal defense of white supremacy and an IQ monopoly, Riordan decided to quote Bishop John F. O'Hara, then presiding over the Army and Navy Diocese. In view of the wholesale racial segregation in the armed forces at that time, I assumed that his all-white experience at Notre Dame had qualified him for his military assignment.

Bishop O'Hara stumbled into the old "some of my best friends" cliché by writing that: "I believe I should tell you frankly that while the faculty [of Notre Dame] has no objection to colored students . . . there are so many southern students at Notre Dame that I feel certain a colored student would find himself in an embarrassing situation if he were to enter here."

Giving himself absolution and doubtless feeling shriven, Bishop O'Hara went on: "We northern Catholics naturally deplore any such thing as race discrimination, but at the same time we have to recognize the feeling of these southern boys with whom race prejudice is strong." It seems incredible that a primate in the Catholic hierarchy, trained in the niceties of logic and the natural law, could not perceive the conflict shaped by his own words. Deploring racism, at the same time he felt he had to "recognize the feeling of these southern boys with whom race prejudice is strong." He was obviously blind to the kind of moral leadership that gave recognition and approval to strong racial prejudice.

Continuing to urge fallacy upon fallacy, the Bishop went on: "The Catholic Church has been very weak in the South, and these prejudices have been gathered from other sources than the Church." Perhaps. But those prejudices were clearly being fostered by America's most famous Catholic university. Indeed, the Bishop strayed into the ridiculous when he fully supported the continued admission of bigots to the university and "training them for a broad Catholic outlook."

He did offer some rather dim hope that "in the course of time, if we get enough Catholics among the white population of the South, they may be able to influence some change of heart among their fellows." Apparently, he meant the white "fellows" in the South, not those at Notre Dame, where their race prejudices had been nurtured, approved, and reinforced.

The case for a change of white hearts, under the circumstances, seemed rather bleak. In the final paragraph of the O'Hara meditation, he apparently threw up his hands in a let's-stand-pat gesture, concluding that: "In the meantime, we have to make the most of the situation as it stands." As though this confession by a famous university of its sociological impotence was insufficient, Father Riordan, abandoning quotatons of others, resorted to historical references. He deplored the "unfortunate circumstances under which the Negro originally came to this country," and revealed something of what he must have believed was an allowable Catholic liberalism. He wrote that it was "taking a discouragingly long time to build up a fair and unbiased attitude towards" the Negro.

Despite the admission that Notre Dame had to cater to the racial prejudices of its southern students, Father Riordan offered the assurance that "Catholic institutions . . . have been and are becoming more active on behalf of our Negro citizens." In proof of that boast, he reached into his personal family archives to cite his grandfather. Riordan wrote: "My grandfather, an Irish immigrant to the South, freed his only colored servant when he came to Indiana, and gave her forty acres of land as a wedding gift." While he described his grandfather's slave as a "servant," obviously, there was no need to "free" a mere servant, as opposed to one held in bondage. That the good and generous grandfather owned at least one slave revealed that he, too, made the most of the situation as it then stood.

Father Riordan's pride in family allowed him to say that his father served in the Union Army, as though his father had volunteered precisely to support abolition. Adopting the Bishop O'Hara posture of making "the most of the situation as it stands," Father Riordan assured me that he had "a sympathetic understanding of your situation" and that his "hope is sincere that our efforts toward justice in this matter may eventually bear fruit." Strange fruit, indeed.

Notre Dame had probably forgotten about its statement of policy made to me so many years ago, but I followed both

Princeton and Notre Dame whenever either was mentioned in the press or magazines. In the summer of 1945, I was still in the First Infantry Division, stationed in Germany, near where the division had been as the war ended. In June of that year, I had written to Notre Dame, asking if its racial policies had changed. The registrar by that time was Father James W. Connerton. He wrote that he could easily understand why Father Riordan's "fine, honest letter" quoted Bishop O'Hara's patient dictum that "We have to make the most of the situation as it stands."

He then said that Notre Dame had "three Negroes in attendance. . . now and last semester we had a fourth." He added that, "We are very fond of these four men and from all appearances they are very happy at Notre Dame." An application blank was enclosed for my convenience.

A *New York Times* article in its edition of February 7, 1949, quoted the Rev. Robert H. Sweeney, the executive assistant to Notre Dame's president, as saying, "The University of Notre Dame maintains today as in the past, a policy of non-discrimination regardless of race, color or creed." This was a lie, of course.

In 1949, apparently, southern white students and blacks from the South, were so comfortable with each other that they enjoyed membership in the Rebel's Club and, as the article noted, "there have been no known incidents."

Both Princeton and Notre Dame were all male in the 1940s. Neither can claim that they voluntarily accepted black students. It was not an easy time for all-male colleges, what with the draft taking millions of men into the military. It was the military, such as with the Navy's V-12 Program, that sent black sailors to various universities which previously had none. It must have been of some economic solace to Princeton and Notre Dame that the government was sending students whose tuition was assured.

ON TO VIRGINIA STATE— AND LINCOLN UNIVERSITY

Deprived of both famous institutions, I found that life at Virginia State was oppressive. The president, John M. Gandy, was a pompous little accommodationist who was adept at making the most of the situation as it then stood and very much the clone of the Notre Dame fathers. This may have been because, intellectually, his mind had never been fully emancipated, much less his analysis of the "place" of the Negro. He was one of the thirteen children of former slaves in Mississippi. His most radical outburst appears to have been changing his middle name, which he disliked, from "Mumphis" to Manuel. When he became president of the college after 1914, he also changed the name from Virginia Normal and Industrial Institute to "Virginia State College for Negroes." He accomplished wonderful things for a segregated society, but remained suspicious of the intentions of the virile young male students toward the nubile beauties at the college. He was the author of a so-called Blue Book that defined the celibate distances that were to be maintained between the sexes. Despite the fact that it was a state-financed college, Gandy's Christian morals commanded that each student must attend chapel, and attendance was carefully monitored. Presumably, such a religious imposition was to assure a virtuous census at the college. Just the opposite was achieved, however, and there were many safaris to Petersburg and places there where the students' concupiscent passions could be expressed.

The Blue Book was known as Gandy's Folly, although it occurred to me that his greater folly was the establishment of a Religion Week on the campus. This was a time when seven different theologians, all Protestant, came to the campus and preached at chapel to an audience mandated to be there.

By this time, I had read the A. Conan Doyle book, *Around the Red Lamp*, and I believed that if such a gifted writer and doctor could reject formal religion as an emotional myth, so could I. As a columnist on the college paper, I had begun to poke fun at the Christians who hated Jews while forgetting that without Judaism there could be no Christianity—not to mention the fact that Christ was a Jew and a rabbi. Presumably, God, the putative father of Jesus, was also Jewish. Since I signed my columns simply, "Peasant," there was no danger that Aunt Catherine would realize that I had betrayed all her early teachings. So far as I ever knew, she had never learned that usually the pittance she had given me for Sunday school had been diverted to the purchase of Tootsie-Rolls.

Thus, Religion Week became my prey. In the heart of the Bible Belt, a greater folly than Religion Week is to poke fun at religion. I managed to insert a headline in the campus paper, saying, "Religion Weak," accusing the touring preachers of "minding their speeches, instead of speaking their minds," despite press stories about the deadly scandal of lynchings of Negroes by pious Christians. In any event, it has remained a mystery to me how Negroes could so enthusiastically adopt the religion of the slaveowners. Of the seven preachers, one was well known to me, Reverend Iams of Harlem's St. James Presbyterian Church. His son and I had occasionally played tennis and I wished to say hello to him. On the day he was scheduled, I decided to attend chapel. I arrived fresh from a tennis court, sweaty and in my shorts, with a towel around my neck and my racquet in hand. This caused some audible comment from the well-dressed students who apparently assumed that God demanded one's Sunday best when in a place of worship.

Within ten minutes, Jefferson, the college football coach, known as "Big Jeff," along with the Dean of Men, one Boone, arrived at my seat. Without preliminary formalities, they lifted me bodily from my seat. I protested with mock piety that I was in God's house and entitled to freedom of religion. I demanded that they unhand me and get themselves to a place of penitence while repeating loud *mea culpas*. They pretended not to hear. I was carried to my dormitory. They confirmed the campus suspicion that the college authorities had keys to our rooms when they unlocked my door and deposited me on my bed. While Big Jeff guarded the door, Boone packed my trunk with things he believed to be mine. They then walked me to the administration building, where an emergency session of the Guidance Committee had been convened. One of my columns had earlier accused the Committee of waving a banner that bore the legend, "In Guide We Trust." The college was not amused, but the authorities were seldom amused by what I believed was typical undergraduate conduct.

It was not my first appearance before the Committee, but it was my first in tennis shorts. Earlier, in a protest against the Blue Book rules defining relations between the sexes (not the kind that took place off campus), I had stuffed some long drawers with scrap paper, painted facial features of agony at the top and, late one night, the effigy was hung, with a table knife through the heart, complete with red ink seeming to be blood. My roommate then called a female student and asked her to look out at the dangling figure near a woman's dormitory. Suddenly, there were loud screams by those who believed they were witnessing a student's suicide. My roommate had spread the rumor that a very sensitive young woman and poet had failed English Lit.

The mystery of the hangman was quickly solved, for many of the wastebasket papers bore my name, including the envelopes from letters sent by Aunt Catherine. That had resulted in a session with the Guidance Committee, where I had been quizzed about my background, and asked how I could betray my early Christian upbringing, if I was reared in the right way, and on and on. I responded to none of the questions, except to say that if there was freedom of religion, surely there was also freedom not to be religious and— for a Negro—absolute freedom not to have the same religion as the slaveowners. The new session with the committee was fairly brief. This allowed Big Jeff and Boone a respite from their weightlifting chores. Indeed, they abandoned their dramatic carrying act and simply escorted me to Big Jeff's car. Followed by the curious stares of students, the car drove off to the railroad station in Petersburg, where I was placed on a train to New York in the Jim Crow car, of course. Watched over carefully until Richmond, I was on my own thereafter.

This caused some strain in my relationships with my parents and Aunt Catherine, who must have begun to think that I was cursed in some way. Rejected by both the white Protestants of Princeton and the separate-but-equal white Catholics, and now by the people of a college of my own "kind" as Heermance had recommended, there I was, once again, at loose ends. It was certainly a tribute to the respect for education that my family had that they did not give up on me. It was a humbling lesson in family values.

James Moore, a Lincoln University graduate with whom I occasionally played tennis, said that my conduct revealed a taste for rabble-rousing and that Lincoln's all-male campus would be a perfect place for me. Without hesitation, an application was made to Lincoln. That university was founded in 1854, as the first college in America for the education of "poor but ambitious colored boys." I was pretty swiftly aging out of the "boy" category and I had never been certain about my ambitions, but I really wished to show my family that I *could* be a well-behaved student. At least, *their* ambition for me was a firm one. Lincoln's curriculum was solidly classical, featuring Latin and Greek and the sciences. With a Lincoln degree, you were qualified to attend a seminary, or a more realistic place such as a medical or law school. Lincoln had been founded by graduates of the Princeton Theological Seminary. During my first interview with a Reverend William Dodge, he proved that he had read my rather tawdry dossier by assuring me that Princeton's seminary had no relationship whatsoever with the town's university. He went on endlessly about the influence of God in all that we do, even suggesting that God had a purpose in permitting Hitler to have the influence he was then exercising in Europe.

In the midst of his rambling sermon, I had despaired of Lincoln. But Dodge, as though concluding that I probably needed the spiritual rehabilitation that a Lincoln education could achieve, surprised me by saying that the required essay I had submitted, along with some of my poetry, revealed that I had long ago been "gloriously" infected by the will of God and that Lincoln and I would be good for each other.

Dodge recommended my acceptance and, except for necessary paperwork, I was accepted. In September 1940, I went off to Lincoln's rural acreage 135 miles from New York, near the Mason-Dixon Line that, in my mind, suggested all of the racial terror of the Confederacy and that period of reimposed slave conditions known as Reconstruction. Lincoln had been a stop on the Underground Railroad as escaped slaves fled to Canada. Unlike its present development as a unit of Pennsylvania's state university system, there was a marvelous sense of uncrowded space. Lincoln Hall, where I was assigned, was almost a hundred years old. My room had a fireplace, beneath which my roommate and I discovered a forgotten cache of rifles and ammunition, now in the university's museum.

My roommate, a tough-talking native of the Bronx, never lost his suspicions about the countryside. The college was near a tiny town called Oxford. Despite that classic name, it was filled with unenlightened bigots, who apparently feared the presence of so many young black men. There had never been more than 400 students there at any one time. Lincoln had its own town, if it could be called that. It was really a mini-village, located about a quarter of a mile from the main campus. It was called Lincoln University,

Pennsylvania. I never saw anything there that could be called a street. Its population was all white. The whites who lived there shopped in nearby Oxford and went to its modest theater. There were always a few white students from the village and even from Oxford at the movie theater in Oxford which was rigidly segregated, if any blacks wished to attend. No medical facilities there would serve blacks, thus making a mockery of the Hippocratic oath's definition of ethics for the profession.

The hospital in Oxford would, of course, accept no black patients—a fact I was soon to learn when a car in which I was riding turned over. All five of its passengers were injured. One of them, as it developed, had a fractured skull. He lay unconscious for several hours until an ambulance could arrive from the University of Pennsylvania Hospital. Lincoln had an affiliation with Penn that was benevolent in its concept, but awkwardly impractical, since life could be imperiled while an ambulance traveled the fifty-five miles from Philadelphia, and then made the return trip. There was, of course, a resident physician on the campus, but his facilities were primitive at best and on weekends, when so many student accidents occurred, he was nowhere to be found.

I found Lincoln students to be a brilliant group of young men, all of whom seemed to focus on ambitions in one profession or another, but mainly medicine or law. Thurgood Marshall, Franklin H. Williams, and Robert Carter all graduated with honors and went on to distinguished records as heroic lawyers in the dangerous civil rights work on the NAACP during the thirties and forties. It was Frank Williams, a year ahead of me, whose unspoken influence persuaded me to study law. He was a born leader and the only person in my life with whom I had a long and lasting friendship. I admired him greatly for his bold insights and his fearless confrontations with white society. It was typical of Frank that when he discovered that he was doomed by cancer, he summoned his friends to a last birthday party for a joyous farewell, a kind of Thanksgiving for the life he had had. It was only after the party that his guests learned its purpose. Had I known the purpose of the party, I would have made an exception to my determination never to attend a party, birthday or otherwise.

(Frank spoke to me on the day he was to leave the hospital for the last time. We arranged to visit, but he died the next day. His last public service had been as the head of a Commission appointed by Governor Mario Cuomo to investigate racism in the courts of New York. I was one of several black judges who testified before the Commission. However, that was long after I was at Lincoln.)

In 1941, all of us then in college and eligible to be drafted learned of the devastation at Pearl Harbor caused by the Japanese air raid. I was then struggling with a burdensome catalog of courses, seeking to cram extra hours of work so that I might graduate before being taken by the military. Virginia State College had refused to send my credits to Lincoln. I had been compelled to start from the beginning, being credited with some hours after being examined. I was reminded of Alexander Hamilton, who arrived in America from Nevis in the British West Indies and sought to be examined to see where he would fit at Princeton. However, the university trustees rejected his application and he entered Kings College (Columbia) in 1793 "upon his own terms." It was only after World War II that I discovered the unpaid "debt" that Virginia State College claimed it was owed by my parents. It was no more than the $9.50 it had cost for my ticket from Petersburg to New York. My rationale, of course, was that I never asked for such a ticket and charging my family was little different from demanding that slaves pay for their unsought transportation to an American plantation.

I left Lincoln in 1942, believing the gossip that I would not be drafted if I was a graduate student. I enrolled at Fordham University's Law School, where Frank Williams was then distinguishing himself. Shortly after my first semester, I was drafted. It was fifty years later when I picked up my college degree, enjoined to do so by Lincoln's president, the first and only woman to occupy that office in the 141 years of its existence. The formerly all-male university had become coed, undergoing many, many changes. I was awarded an honorary degree before I received my Bachelor of Science.

Ill-equipped to become a soldier, I had long resisted the dictates of authority. I called myself a pacifist. I deplored the rigid racial segregation in the military and my entire family feared that I would not fare well in the army. As events proved, they were right.

INTO THE ARMY—AND MARRIAGE

PATRIA

they will play at
angry hide-and-seek
on some wet and coded shore
and before their sweat of
marching dries,
they will be daggered
in their rows,
but loyal cheers will goad them on
with loyalty to join the dead,
then, we who scavenge in
all the wondrous words of praise
will praise the passion of our cause
as we weed among the murder of our crop

— BW

When I was ordered to report to my draft board, I was living at 43 West 66th Street, in one of the two houses on that Manhattan block reserved for black tenants. The houses, numbers 43 and 45, were owned by a black Baptist church organization. They were five story walkup buildings. Forty-three was next to a riding academy, where indoor polo was played, and where I could earn a few dollars walking ponies after their exertions in a game. On the other side of the building was a garage. The neighborhood was a busy one, with an armory on the opposite side of the street and several ballet studios. I lived next door to Katharine Dunham, the dancer, whose apartment was bare of furniture in her living room, except for an enormous radio-phonograph on which she played recorded music as she taught her classes. Now and then, my roommate and I shared a hot dog, coffee, or tea with her.

The only air conditioner in the building was owned by the resident superintendent, a man named Foster. Seemingly stern and severe, he was an exception to the generally-held view that superintendents were all heavy drinkers and heedless of their duty. Mr. Foster was meticulous in his work. His wife told fortunes and appeared to have an impressive clientele, mostly white. During summer heat waves, I often slept on the roof. It was a wonderful location. Both my roommate and I could walk to work. Both of us had night classes, he at Fordham College and I at the law school, then located on the twenty-eighth floor of the Woolworth Building. My roommate, Jim Moss, worked on Seventh Avenue near 57th Street, and I worked in an art gallery on East 57th Street for fifteen dollars per week, including a half day on Saturdays. The draft would take me away from all of that, the kind of relaxed happiness I would never thereafter know. I would miss the left wing and Marxist speakers who gathered in Columbus Circle. I would also miss the meetings at St. Nicholas Arena on the corner of 66th Street and Broadway, where one would hear folksingers Pete Seeger and Josh White, among others, including those who were asking for contributions of canned goods and other foods for striking dockworkers on the West Side.

At college, I was known as a conscientious objector, but I had no real knowledge of what such an objector was. I did know that I did not like war or the military and I suspected that I would not be a good soldier, or even an acceptable one. I had prepared a little speech for the director of my draft board, in opposition to segregation in the armed services. I thought that if I were angry enough and loud enough, I might be rejected. In answer to my written declaration that I was a conscientious objector, my draft board had replied swiftly, asking me to document the religious connections that would satisfy the military's requirements for such status. Denying religion and condemning it as one of the primary causes of world discord, and having agitated against Christianity, I regrettably had no religious basis to support my position.

My draft board was in the West 63rd Street YMCA. I reported as requested. When my name was called, I walked to the desk manned by an old veteran. Without any preliminaries, I said "America has examined me and found me fit to fight for democracy; I have examined democracy and found it not fit to be fought for." The draft board director, who had kept his head down during my firmly delivered remarks, looked up and asked, "What did you say, soldier?" With the timidity of a first-year law student arguing against reality, I simply gave my name. I was promptly shipped off to Fort Dix, where drill sergeants began a process geared toward humiliating anyone who had gone beyond grade school. When a sergeant asked the members of my group of recruits how many had gone to college, there was an eager display of hands, as though they knew that such an intellectual accomplishment would yield an instant reward, or command of at least a battalion of lesser souls. They were told to stand together, aside from the other draftees. The sergeant then went on down the line, from high school graduates, to high-school dropouts and to those who had dropped out even before high school. He then ordered the college graduates to pick up cigarette butts, papers, and trash, while the others supervised.

My roommate, Jim Moss, drafted before I was, had been at Fort Dix for some time. He found me to warn me to keep my mouth shut, advising that I should forget wisecracks, puns, and jokes. He said that most of the people in charge were white southerners and he wanted me to avoid serious "misunderstandings and trouble." He then said it would be a disaster if I were sent to the South for basic training. He told me that no matter how often my name was called for a shipment, I should simply stay in my barracks. He wanted to make certain that I would not be sent south. For six weeks, I remained in the barracks, no matter how often my name was called and, on weekends, Jim and I commuted between Fort Dix and Manhattan.

And then, one day, Jim came to me and whispered that he had succeeded in placing me on a shipment that was going to Buffalo and I should report when my name was called. I did as I was told, and whispered to anyone who would listen that we were being shipped to Buffalo. That rumor, of course, spread rapidly, with the black soldiers smiling knowingly. We were taken to a long train and away we went. The train rolled through Philadelphia, arousing some suspicions about the rumor. Next, came Wilmington, Baltimore, and Washington, and then on into the deep South. My reputation as a rumor-monger was destroyed, and so was I. The train finally stopped in a hinterland town called Dothan, Alabama, where trucks took us to Fort Rucker, soon rechristened Fort Mother Rucker.

The next day, a Captain Hopke greeted us. He was

white. I was to learn that all of the officers were white in the quartermaster battalion to which we had been assigned. I also learned that the all-black quartermaster units were, among ourselves, known as laborers. Captain Hopke proudly stated that he was from a town called Sikeston, Missouri. I was immediately shocked and dismayed. In 1942, Sikeston had been in the news for lynching a black man who had been difficult to kill. He had been beaten, instead of hanged from a tree, and he seemed to refuse to die, no matter how brutal the assault upon his body. Finally, he was dragged behind the bumper of a car through the streets of Sikeston. I was amazed that anyone would advertise that his home was such a place. Hopke, I was to discover, had a quick temper.

He said he wanted particularly to greet the shipment of "you boys," since he understood that most of us had been in college. He expected, he said, to have a first-class company. He ordered us to line up. We did, in an inexpert way, so to speak. Hopke said he would walk along our line; that he would pause before each one of us and we were to salute smartly and give our names and dogtag numbers as they appeared on our service records. Still smarting from having been dragooned into the army while still a law student, I gave Hopke an exactitude that did not please him. As he paused before me, I saluted and said, "Wright, Bruce McM., 32955618, Paren. Col. close Paren. That means colored." Hopke was livid. His eyes burned into mine as he said through tight lips that he was not going to have any "smartasses" in his outfit. "But," I said, "that's exactly how it appeared on my service record." Hopke glared and turned us over to a hulking first sergeant, a leftover from World War I, who would become a part of my daily life at Fort Rucker. He had witnessed the entire incident between Hopke and me. He drew me aside, after Hopke had departed and told me he had been in the army for twenty-five years and that I wasn't "gonna live long with your attitude."

I told my fellow captives that the army had doubly insulted us, first by segregating us and again by assigning us to a company headed by a man from a community that had lynched at least one Negro. They merely laughed, saying I should be careful. Naturally, the first sergeant heard about some of the things I was saying. One Sunday, when things were rather quiet and most of the battalion's soldiers had passes to escape from the dry county in which Fort Rucker was located to the available alcohol of nearby Panama City, Florida, First Sergeant Johnson asked me to follow him. Johnson was at least six feet five and well over two hundred pounds. He was never without a policeman's nightstick. He led me to his office and directed me to sit down. He told me that he had not had much "schoolin'" but that he had "mother smarts." Otherwise, he added, he never would have become a first sergeant, making the same pay as any white top sergeant. He confessed that he could neither read nor write and that he wanted me to help him so I could keep out of trouble. Each morning, he said, I was to read to him the orders of the day. He would commit them to memory, literally, as I read them to him. Each morning, he would stand in front of the men, just before they exercised, and, holding up the orders as though he was reading them, he mouthed exactly what I had read to him.

He had other duties for me as well. He wanted me to wake the bugler each morning and to write letters for him. In exchange, I would be allowed to ignore most formations and marches. He pointed out a vacant barracks where I could spend most of my time. He gave me an ancient typewriter and lots of paper. I thus began a rather lazy career, writing love letters to his mistresses, widely strewn throughout the country wherever he had served through the years and, of course, to his wife. "Save the best for her," he said, with a flash of redemptive loyalty. With the luxuries of time, a typewriter, and paper, I could write my own letters and type and retype the poetry that I had been writing since my days on Cape Cod after high school. It was a satisfactory arrangement from every point of view, except, possibly, Hopke's. But Hopke needed Johnson and Johnson knew it and he knew, also, just how far he could go with Hopke. "I seen his type all over this country and in the Philippines, too. I traveled in all them places."

Once my letters for Johnson were written, I was busy writing my own letters to Adam Clayton Powell, Jr., then the first Negro member of the New York City Council. I wanted to escape from Fort Rucker and compete for a place with the then forming all-Negro pilots in training at Tuskegee, Alabama. It seemed such an easy thing at the time, a simple transfer from one unit to another, both in Alabama. As I was to learn later, my letters never left the post. I was trapped. It seemed I was needed right where I was.

The first sergeant thought that since I was a law student when drafted, I would make an excellent medic. I was assigned to the battalion surgeon, where I became a clerk, spared the usual drudgery of basic training, and with easy access to typewriters. One night, the black troops were routed out to help put out a fire started earlier by the target practice of a white artillery group on the post. I asked to see Captain Hopke. The first sergeant told me to be careful and watch my mouth. "What is it, now, Wright?" the captain greeted me. I began to tell Hopke that I could not help put out the fires. He yelled "What!" I began to tell him that the trees of Alabama and neighboring states were too tragically involved with the lynchings of Negroes and that it would be a sociological boon to the country if they all burned down. Again, the captain seemed on the verge of a stroke or heart attack. He yelled, "I'm giving you a direct order. Get the hell out of here and fight those fires." "Sir," I began, only to be cut off by the captain's angry scream to the first sergeant: "Take him to the stockade, Johnson; he's on charges; he's guilty of insubordination. I'm tired of his crap."

That was military justice. I was guilty, but still to be tried before a martial court. I was led away by Sergeant Johnson, who muttered as we walked, saying, "I told you to watch your mouth, damn it." Naturally, I believed my first year law class training could enable me to handle the crisis and I elected to represent myself, even though an officer was assigned to be my counsel. He was not a lawyer, but I must have thought that I was. The trial was hardly that. The charges were read and the prosecuting officer placed Hopke on the witness stand and asked him what happened. Hopke's recall was not in conflict with my own. I cross-examined the captain, asking him, first, if he was aware of any lynchings of Negroes anywhere in America. The prosecuting officer, naturally, objected and was sustained. I then asked if he was aware of the lynching of a Negro in his home town of Sikeston, Missouri. Again, an objection was sustained. I had the feeling that my efforts to bring a sociological perspective to Fort Rucker were not prospering.

In the end, I reserved my propaganda for summation. The all-officer members of the tribunal simply listened, shaking their heads. Within minutes of the concluding statements, the panel returned a verdict of guilty. I was lectured on the importance of unquestioning obedience to an officer's orders and the seriousness of the offense of insubordination. It was an old story, I suppose, for the people at Virginia State had also accused me of insubordination and Aunt Catherine had said over and over to me that my mouth would be my undoing. The presiding colonel said he would take into consideration the brevity of my time in the military, and my general inexperience. He warned that any such repeated conduct could result in a sentence of years and a dishonorable discharge. I was sentenced to sixty days in the stockade, at hard labor. Fortunately for me, before my induction, I had been running with the New York Pioneer Club and I was in excellent physical condition. Hard labor is a sobering experience. I resolved, not to stop bitching and complaining, but to be more careful. But I did not help put out the fires.

It was some three months later when I had my next conflict, barely thirty days after being released from the stockade. Recreation for Negro troops on the post meant occasional movies in the gym in our area. Enlisted men operated the projector and their general ineptness guaranteed that the film would often slip out of alignment or break. At such times, the gym would be in an uproar of vulgar insults yelled at the projection team. In the dark gym, freedom of speech meant unidentified expressions of insults and obscene references to the mothers of the men operating the projector. In the midst of the noise and obscenities, I stood up on my chair and in the most deep and pompous voice I could summon, I said, loudly, "At ease, men! This is General Nuisance speaking, and I have beside me my adjutant, Major Problem . . ." And the lights came on over the hushed soldiers. There I was, standing on my chair. Once again, Sergeant Johnson was told to trundle me off to the stockade to await charges. This time, the charges were that I was impersonating an officer. I thought that defending against such charges would be a snap. At my trial, I demanded that the prosecutor produce the general it was said I was impersonating. The prosecuting officer dropped the charge of impersonating Major Problem, saying that, after all, that was precisely what I was. The panel of my officer jurors allowed the trace of a smile to relax their grim faces at that mention. In the end, the officers must have realized how ridiculous the charges were, because they found that I was guilty and my penalty was a week's extra duty. That could be whatever the first sergeant wanted. And what he wanted was more flowery correspondence to his nationwide network of concubines.

It had occurred to me some time before, long before being drafted, that I was not the stuff from which good soldiers are made. I was unhappy with what I felt was my intellectual and physical isolation and with the possibility that the war would never end. Only country or religious music was played on the post by the enlisted men's radios. One soldier did allow me to listen on Sundays to Arturo Toscanini and the NBC Symphony, for which, as our company's resident entrepreneur, he charged me $10, one-third of my monthly income as a private. I began to brood about how it was all coming out, assuring myself that I would feel much more manly and heroic as a soldier if I were in a combat unit. I was fooling myself, because I believed that war was sheer folly and that powerful world leaders simply did not have the IQ to deal with world problems in a civilized way and thus resorted to force. The truth has been defined as the say-so of the leader having the greatest deadly power.

In the midst of my melancholia, we black laborers left

Fort Rucker and headed for New York, amid rumors that we were going to embark for England. I almost felt free. We arrived at Camp Kilmer and I immediately went AWOL with several others from New York. The looseness of security was reflected in how easy it was to walk through the February snow, go over a fence and head for a bus to New York. It was an incredible change from Fort Rucker. There, whenever black troops were given a furlough, they had to report to camp headquarters from which they then could head for Dothan and the train station. Sometimes, black soldiers would remain at headquarters for two or three days, using up furlough time and going nowhere because they had to wait until all of the white troops were accommodated by the limited transportation facilities. Then the Negroes would be allowed to ride out, sitting in the back of a bus. I had once been pulled from a bus on the Rucker post itself because I refused to sit in the back to ride to the post hospital to see a friend. The MP on duty said he was from New York also, but he would crack my head as soon as look at me if I did not move to the rear. I walked the rest of the way.

Leaving Kilmer, my first visit was to Connie Gray, whom I had been seeing while I was a student at Lincoln. She was really the first girlfriend I ever had. She was a brilliant student of science at Hunter College and would go on to do secret graduate work at Princeton and the University of Pennsylvania. After that, she did further highly secret work at army communications laboratories near Red Bank, New Jersey. (She refused to tell me the nature of her work and to this day, she has not told me.) Despite my endangered status as an AWOL, we walked in Central Park and sat on a bench. A passing elderly woman gave us a disapproving look. Later,

I wrote a poem about the incident.

> *Madam, you are astonished to behold warm lovers*
> *on this cold bench in February;*
> *but we are young and cannot abide*
> *the unsure sign of groundhogs*
> *or touring robins.*
> *A long war makes all life short;*
> *do not begrudge us this tiny cup that*
> *runneth over;*
> *for the future is filled with neuters*
> *and we have found that the bitter is*
> *most bitter and that sweetness*
> *is the acid of one swift moment*
> *too soon swallowed up as the past.*
> *Madam, you are old, but we are young;*
> *you have your tidy array of archived memories*
> *and time to thumb through albums of*
> *your past-tense daring.*
> *We have but now and our love,*
> *so move on into your vault of memory,*
> *let staid footfalls of your thoughts there*
> *echo some by-gone revel,*
> *some proper indiscretion for timid recollection,*
> *but we are young—*
> *forgive us this impertinent kiss.*

In the mood at that time, however, we discussed mar-

riage. Connie said that if we did not do it before I went overseas, we might never do it. With that prologue and no
prospects for the kind of life that marriage usually antici-
pates, we decided to get married as quickly as possible. I
picked up the County Clerk's forms to waive the waiting
period after the blood test and called Shelby Albright Rooks,
the Lincoln professor who had given me the lowest grade I
ever received there. He was a Presbyterian minister who had
taught a course in religion; our debates had not pleased him.
I was the class infidel, he said. He was then married to
Dorothy Maynor, the singer whose voice, Arturo Toscanini
said, had the tones of a "dark cello." I never knew whether
the color of the cello had anything to do with Ms. Maynor's
race. I located my old adversary, in his wife's Carnegie Hall
apartment. He debated the possibility of performing the marriage there, but decided he would do it in his study at St.
James Presbyterian Church—much to my dismay, over the
church setting, not the marriage. Rooks had been the Class
Adviser for the Class of 1942 at Lincoln. I thought it proper
for one of my enemies to perform the marriage.

In his letter to the members of the Class of 1942, Rooks
had advised against despair and "snap judgments;" yet, here
I was, on the brink of exercising a snap judgment and inviting
him as a co-conspirator. Despite the letter's injunction to the
class to broaden its "views of life, of man, of God," he uttered
a rhyme that suggested doom. I remain intrigued by the two
lines, a heroic couplet that he quoted without author attribu-
tion:

> *"Love is no more, and justice is a lie;*
> *Life is a cheat — and we fare forth to die."*

He was in effect telling us, in a little different way, what Alan Seager told us before he went off to perish for his country when he wrote, "I have a rendezvous with death/At some disputed barricade." In view of my then imminent departure overseas during the height of the War, the brooding of one known and one unknown poet rankled in my mind.

A day or so later, before the ceremony, Connie was subdued and said nothing, until asked by Rooks if she was sure she wished to go ahead, just as though I was to be a combat soldier instead of a noncombatant medic in a labor battalion. As I later learned, Connie was gravely concerned about what her father might do when he discovered our marriage. I was not one of his favorites. While I was still at college, I had come one weekend to take Connie to a Town Hall concert. I arrived in my little Model A Ford two-seater with rumble seat, and a broken window on the passenger side. It was raining. In the Gray apartment, I chatted with her mother, whom I dearly loved. Her father said little or nothing to me. He was a rather elegant man, tall and handsome and reputed to have at least one mistress on every block where he delivered mail. A black postman, in those days, was a person of consequence. He was straightlaced, a veteran of World War I who still kept and polished some of his genuine leather equipment from 1917. A longtime member of the 369th Infantry Regiment, he had had a distinguished record in combat in France. Indeed, France had accepted the black soldiers when General Pershing had refused to use them under American command. Mr. Gray was known as the "Governor" and that was what I called him at all times when I spoke to him. He detested my habit of wearing sneakers year-round and shorts during the summer, especially on Sunday. We were not friends. Connie clearly adored her father.

Just as we were about to leave for Town Hall, I remembered that the passenger-side window was broken and I asked Connie to bring a towel. Her father yelled, "What!" It was as though I had screamed that I had made his daughter pregnant. I had no idea what he was so excited about. It was only years later that I learned that lovers took a towel to aid in the comfort of making love. Both Connie and I were virgins and the sophisticated use of a towel on a date had never occurred to me and the Governor's angry excitement was a complete mystery. In retrospect, it was more a comment on his own sexual frivols than those he was willing to attribute to me.

Now, when Connie and I stood in the study of Reverend Rooks, her continued reservation and concern were because she had told neither her father nor her mother that she was going to be married that day, much less the place or time of the event. Neither had I told anyone. The marriage was performed with the usual priestly advices and cautious assurances that I would surely return from the War and have a happy and fruitful marriage. I did return and it was fruitful, but neither of us could know any of that at that time.

The vows exchanged, we took the subway to the 66th Street apartment and, in keeping with whatever I had learned from movies and books, I undressed and jumped in bed, urging Connie to hurry and do the same. When it was dark, I would return to Camp Kilmer the same way I had left. Connie was reluctant. There is probably no situation more inept than two young virgins engaging in a conjugal relationship. Connie began to cry and to deplore the fact that she had not told her parents, especially her father. She had a pain in her back. Heroically, I got dressed and went out to Broadway to find a pharmacy and some aspirin. I walked bravely past the armory, with its guards at the entrance, offering a pleasant greeting, as though I was fully authorized to be walking confidently. I returned, the aspirin was taken—but it changed nothing. I was to return to Camp Kilmer unrequited and the next day, leave for Scotland. I would not see my bride until three years had passed. Our goodbyes were shy, almost formal.

Our labor battalion was loaded aboard a so-called Liberty ship, with the black troops still segregated and consigned to the lowest deck of the vessel. It was hot and close down there and it would get worse as the voyage progressed—slowly it seemed. Seasickness soon took over, with its foul odors of vomit and fear. Captain Hopke must have imagined that he was punishing me, for I was assigned to guard duty topside. It was the best thing about that leisurely February voyage, except for seeing Captain Hopke, green and nauseous, leaning over a rail. There were only two meals a day and each soldier was given two meal tickets. That was that; no ticket, no meal. Seeing Hopke in such painful distress, I asked him, with mock concern, if I might borrow one of his meal tickets, since it seemed rather obvious that he would not be wanted to dine that day. He merely glared, looking more drained than ever. I walked on, trying to show a jaunty pace and even enjoying the fresh air over the cold, gray ocean.

OVERSEAS DUTY

". . . old soldiers never die, their privates just fade away."

— Anon.

The voyage was uneventful, except for those on the one ship in the convoy that was torpedoed, and on ours, the voice of the ship's chaplain over the vessel's public address system. He invited the "colored soldiers" to sing some "darky songs," since he knew "the colored" were such wonderful singers. Even the most benighted of the black troops joined in the loud denigration of the chaplain in cruel and accurate adjectives. After three weeks of crossing the wintery Atlantic that was very much like riding an unruly horse, we came to a port in Scotland called Gurock. From there, we entrained to Glasgow, then Liverpool and, eventually, to Barry, a port town in Wales.

While there, I was given a rough idea of how my fellow soldiers would and did react under a bombing raid from the Germans. Before being assigned to barracks, we were simply in small tents. The Germans bombed the port one night and some of the troops fled in terror, with no idea where they were running. Some ran with tents draped about them. Apparently, they had risen so quickly that their heads poked through the tops of the small tents. It was a hilarious sight for me, as I stood watching and looking for some view of German bombers. I thought that as a member of a labor battalion, that was about as close as I would ever get to combat. I was wrong, as later events would prove.

In Barry, the segregated Red Cross Club was headed by

a white woman, a southerner from Georgia. She was unfazed by the loud energy of the black troops or the nighttime bombing raids of the Germans. I asked her to get a clean set for us and some classical records. She planned a trip to Bristol for shopping. She asked that I accompany her. I was wary. There were always complaints by Red Cross women, especially young ones, that they had been sexually attacked by black soldiers, and convictions, imprisonment, and dishonorable discharges were routine. Jennifer Macbeth seemed to have much pull with the officers. She had secured official permission for me to accompany her to Bristol before she mentioned the trip to me.

We went by train. At one point, the train was in a long tunnel. Ms. Macbeth (she said I must call her Jennifer), clung to me while we were in the darkness. I could not respond to the plain implications of her intimacy. I had heard too much about willing white women being surprised in the arms of black men. They immediately screamed rape. They were always believed. The authorities always believed that blacks were sexually aggressive. I was relieved when the train came into the open.

Jennifer always waited until closing time at the club to say she needed to speak to me about what she could get to entertain the men during their off-time. I was full of good-faith suggestions. She seemed annoyed. One night, when she asked that I stay late, I noticed that she locked the door and put out the lights, except in the corridor of the Nissen hut that led from the club to her private quarters.

She came face to face with me, just staring. "Private Wright," she whispered, "you have such beautiful eyes." She could see nothing of my very ordinary brown eyes. She spoke as in a trance. Was this one of those traps where she would accuse me? Panic immobilized me. Suddenly, she began to undo my belt. Her perfume was like a narcotic. She fumbled with my trousers, undoing the buttons of my fly. She took my member in one hand. In response to her touch, it was clear that my panic was not impotent to her intention.

My trousers dropped over my leggings and onto the floor. She tugged me along the corridor. My steps minced, almost a stumble. She was moaning softly and whispering, "Come, come." And suddenly, I did, all over her hand, skirt, and floor. She stopped, and her tears were a sudden fountain. She looked at me in the dim corridor. Her face was contorted, a picture of pain, as though I had committed some act of cruel torture. She then branded my brain and memory forever as she sat on her knees and leaned against the corridor wall. She spoke clearly, her accent bitter and accusing. "A woman wants to enjoy it, too." She was gazing as though into distant space.

I was humiliated, diminished. Her hurt was a silent scream. She rose slowly, said no other word, and stood by the exit door. I pulled up my trousers, tightened my belt, and left. To this day, I can have no degree of intimacy with a woman, whether in conversation or otherwise, without those words leaping at me from memory like a Halloween apparition.

To believe one's self to be loved by a woman can be the product of arrogance, the self-delusion of happiness, or simply a retreat to the mirage of an oasis in a passionate desert. Still, I believe that three women in my life truly loved me. Jennifer was one. Her correct attitude toward me was painful. She was cheerful and considerate, but never, during the months before D-Day, did she suggest intimacy of any kind. She wore a false face that refused eye contact with me. I was not asked to stay late and help with the club. Now and then, when away from others, as I read a book, she would ask if everything was all right, as though she wished to offer me comfort, the very luxury I had stolen from her.

After I joined the First Infantry Division, I was amazed to find that Jennifer would turn up in a Red Cross truck with coffee and donuts after every combat mission or whenever my regiment was in reserve and given an opportunity to have a cold field-shower. She always seemed happy to see me, begged me to be careful, and behind her truck, she would give me a hasty kiss.

One day in March, near the end of the war, we were in the Hartz Mountains. It was as though spring was trying to mute the conflict. We sat in the sun, looking down into a valley through breaks in the clouds around the heights. "Will you go back to law school?" For the first time since Wales, she looked straight at me. Roused to drama by her concern, I replied, "Of course." After a pause, I added, "If I survive, I mean. Otherwise, I'll go elsewhere." It was always the sophomore in me that could spoil a precious moment.

Suddenly, her eyes seemed on the brink of tears, but there was only a torrent of words. She told me that she knew where I was at all times because one of her relatives was a brigadier general in the First Division, that "Georgia would be different after the war; that her father, now deceased, had been a lawyer in Atlanta, and I could have his books and practice law there. She went on and on as though uttering lyrics for an improbable dream. She said she loved me and my poetry that I had shared with her in Swansea.

For the first time, I told her that I had been married in the morning of the very day that I had been shipped overseas. She appeared to be unaffected by the news, saying that divorces are easy and that her father had handled many. She added that wives of soldiers understood, or had to learn, that emotional estrangement would match the physical distance of separation. She knew this as a social worker, she said. Closeness in the present could overwhelm the past. Older than I was in years and experience, she sounded wise.

My father had married a white woman. I thought that she often treated him with disdain and some contempt, especially when commenting on the noises he made when eating soup. Would I do the same thing as my father? I had already determined that I would not. Jennifer and I kept in touch by writing. While in Wales, she had given my poetry to a T. C. Hart, an editor with Williams Press, a Cardiff publisher. After my experiences with Dean Wicks and his comment on Datus Smith, then head of the Princeton University Press, I had no hopeful expectations about Cardiff. I knew nothing of Hart's efforts until fifty copies of my first book of poetry was delivered to me in France. Five hundred copies had been published, entitled *From the Shaken Tower*. T. C. Hart apologized for only publishing 500 copies, attributing it to the paper shortage in England.

I was thrilled but had no idea what to do with the small books in the field. Jennifer pretended that she was as surprised as I. The news that I had written a book of poetry only reinforced the views of some that I was a homosexual.

After the Hartz Mountains, I was wounded in a rural German town called Altenruthen. I thought my luck was running out. My first wound resulted in my first plane ride. With others, I was flown from France to England. I heard the nurses on the plane speaking of Birmingham. I feared it was Alabama. Remembering how I was pulled from a bus because I sat near the front when I got on and how black soldiers had had to wait until white soldiers boarded transportation to

Dothan, the nearest train station, to begin their furloughs, I was despondent. Sometimes the black troops, holding their two-weeks furloughs, would have to wait two or three days, wasting their liberty time before catching a train, just to allow white troops to use the buses. The plane, of course, landed in England and the other Birmingham.

It was there that I awoke one day to see a black American woman at my bedside. She was in the uniform of the Women's Army Auxiliary. Cheerfully, she informed me that Eisenhower resented the attention black soldiers were enjoying from British women, and he wanted them to fraternize with some "real" women for a change, those of their "own kind." The use of the word "real" was her way of declaring her position, vis-à-vis white women. Her meaning was reinforced when she asked, "Do you prefer English girls? If so, I'll leave."

Ignoring the question, I assured her that I was delighted to see her. "Perhaps we can go dancing tonight." We both smiled at that impossibility. Bright and curious about the world, she said she lived on Quincey Street in Brooklyn. We discussed what a fraud Eisenhower was. "He has a German name you know. I don't really trust him." My own distrust would later be italicized. For the next two weeks, when I did not have conversations with my "own kind," I played chess with a young English boy who took the game seriously and was back every afternoon for either vengeance or another triumph. He was too polite to call it either. One day, in the confidence and joy of a victory, he asked, "What did you do as a civilian?" I told him, almost jokingly, that I was a poet. "Go on," he said, his eyes wide in disbelief. "How could you be a poet and only a private?" While his question showed respect for the status of a poet in his eyes, it reflected no knowledge of America's sociology or its intellectual history

BATTLE-SCARRED

The integration into combat units, I was told, was the result of pressure brought by Eleanor Roosevelt and Benjamin O. Davis, Sr., then a brigadier general and the only black general in the Army. He had been used for the most part to investigate hostile conflict between white and black troops—that is, to keep the blacks cool. He was not much admired by many of us who believed him to be something of a pompous lackey used to keep the Negro soldier in "their place." In any event, the experiment went forward.

Black officers who volunteered had to come to the infantry as privates. The numbers volunteering and the officers willing to abandon their commissions, were an impressive demonstration of the willingness of blacks to forgive the society that had so long scorned them, or an example of how many blacks were ignorant of their own history. For me, it was simple: If we fought for America, the country would make things better for all blacks. I was wrong, of course. Indeed, the experiment, from the viewpoint of my personal experience, did not get off to a good start. The black squad that reported to the Third Battalion of the 26th Regiment, First Infantry Division was greeted by a captain from South Carolina. A small and feisty Confederate, the captain looked at us and snarled, "I never thought I'd live to see the day when a black nigger would wear the Big Red One." For emphasis, he slapped his shoulder patch, a big red number one in a shield-shaped design. I found the gesture as ridiculous as it was melodramatic and jingoistic. I was reminded of the Samuel Johnson assertion that "Patriotism is the last refuge of a scoundrel," and a ridiculous one at that. He would not last beyond the campaign through France.

A black soldier from the tough ghetto of New Haven's Dixwell Avenue bragged to his comrades that he had been the instrument of the captain's death. There was always much bragging after a combat mission. Often, in the general confusion of combat, responsibility for specific acts could not be proven. Quite often, our officers did not know where they were. Once, when my company was under severe enfilading fire, a lieutenant crawled up to me and whispered tensely, "Wright, can you read a map? Where the hell are we?" This happened after we had crossed the Elbe; our brave troops had scattered when fired at, dropping their weapons. We were, it developed, unintentionally, within the German lines. The experience did not reinforce confidence in the officer class, if they were indeed a class.

I had never been an enthusiastic soldier. I hated the enforced allegiance and unreasoned discipline. I had always detested discipline and subordination in nay case, even as I hated the trappings of superiority based on nothing more than white skin. Ever since the Selective Service law had gone into effect and I knew I would be drafted sooner, rather than later, I had thought about the difficulties I would encounter as a soldier. I had read *All Quiet on the Western Front*, and had some false expectations of what to expect in 1942. The Governor, my father-in-law-to-be, had also mentioned how quickly black soldiers had been the victims of courts martial during and after World War I. Playing soldier had never been one of my youthful pleasures. However, if I were to live up to my self-imposed reason for volunteering, I would be compelled to mask my horror of violence and act out the end that I believed black combat troops would achieve: a better life for

Negroes in America. After all, America had been wrested from the Indians in bloody violence. The country's heroes were all achievers in the field of violence and bloodletting. Even the losers, except for Custer, have been venerated as heroes. The outnumbered victims of the Alamo have been given an honored place in military history. Poor Custer, called a fop because of his personal taste in uniforms, obviously underestimated the abilities of the Indians in combat, in an exhibition of white arrogance, the arrogance of self-endowed white superiority.

The landscape of America is dotted with statues of military heroes. Even the Confederate traitors have their honored dead. Richmond, the one-time capital of the Rebels, has its Monument Walk, where the giants of the South's lost cause dramatize the glory of military death and defeat. It must be the same the world over. De Gramont, in his book *The French*, speaks of a true French military hero as someone, such as Vercingetorix, who has lost a war vital to the survival of France.

The blacks, in their dream world of an America being healed of its disease of racism, imagined that their role in combat in a war against Hitler's racism would somehow eliminate American racism. Thinking about it today, I am embarrassed by such a naive view of American society and, indeed, of American history. Many of us worry about how to change things while we remain the same, as though we can celebrate a present tense triumph while capturing past glory, when neither exists. We blacks have cherished such contradictory concerns, despite the fact that the past has only one lonely glory, and that is survival. But it is a past that has been so perilous, so violent, and so shameful that it should not be glorified. Survival, survival has no convenient adjectives.

Still, America's most treasured honors are reserved for violence, the approved murders by the military. Apparently, that is what I, a genuine physical coward, volunteered for in the combat infantry. It was a dangerous drama in which I elected to act, and only I could define my role, although other factors dictated the circumstances in which that role would be acted out. It was *acting*, for I was compelled to mask my essential cowardice and fear of violence by performing stupid deeds with theatrical bravado. No matter how unsung, one can feel that he is heroic simply by surviving, as though survival is an act of self-created magic. Most Americans have no idea what the ravages of war can do to a landscape, other than what they see on their television sets. And no matter how terrifying those visions of destruction and bloodletting are, they are viewed from the comfortable distance of one's home. Some parts of America have, however, been visited by what the faithful call acts of God, acts that if committed by humans, would be felonies. This makes God a repeat felon. But to walk through the wartime stink and destruction of a village, with private secrets strewn like refuse along the streets, is to give sadness its meaning, even for the anonymous occupants of simple homes along the way. It was difficult to imagine such people as unprotesting idolaters of Hitler, of the death camps and the ovens, the concentration camps; but too many were. In a moment of wildly anxious fire and patriotic hate, the labor of an ancient people had been undone and made into litter. It was not easy for me to be proud. In college, I had found an academic companion in the humanities. In the midst of the man-made destruction, I often asked myself what I was doing there.

In a way, I suppose, I was lucky, for one man's view of war is fairly limited and foreshortened. It becomes a primitive painting with a tortured view, a fiery Hieronymous Bosch, with an incomprehensible jumble of menacing haphazard patterns. To get some idea of what one has done, an edition of the military's newspaper had to be read. It was rather like looking for one's own obituary. It all seemed so useless, so much without any of the trappings of civilization. War has a sinister alchemy in reverse, as it changes men into something base, rude, and ruthless, instead of rich and positive. It is a rough blessing since it takes ruthlessness to win wars. We who are in the infantry are the dregs of humanity. The officers never care how many such soldiers they must sacrifice. After an action, I have heard them bragging. They invoke the arrogant grammar of their survival, placing a false face on their terror. They reflect on what they have done and how it was superior to what the enemy has done. It is a way to uncoil the crouching instinct and the fear they hope does not show. They worry that the dead of the enemy look pretty much the same as their own.

There may be a seeming murderous sameness about every day and every night, but the raucous history of war never repeats itself; the same frustrations may be repeated because man is man and seems to stumble into the same pitfalls of stupidity age after age. But every action represents a new and different kind of terror. Despite this, there are moments when soldiers can gleefully shoot at the fleeing enemy as though firing at painted ducks at a Coney Island concession. As an innocent student of the humanities I remained appalled as I regarded myself each day of combat. I came to believe that my thick books of philosophy were little more than false inventions that ignored the truth of the physical for the sake of the mind. War pulls the scab off genteel pretensions and reveals man's close kinship with life and death in a rude jungle. War is terrible, brutal and unhuman; its winners are simply survivors who become the champion killers of the world.

For me, war can be summed up as a cold, sunny day in a quiet village on a stream, a village that explodes as I enter. It is filled with terrifying sounds that give pain its sharpest meaning. It is the sound of shattering glass and a man yelling with his last, surprised question: "Who the hell was the son of a bitch who shot me like that?" as though there are good ways to shoot another human being. And yet, no matter how frightening a battle, there are always the braggart survivors, the bully boys who know how to ignore the mortal arithmetic by which those around him have become the statistics of loss. The survivors speak loudly and enthusiastically about the conflict, forgetting for a moment in the glory and miracle of being alive how frightened they had been, how filled with dread. They wanted to communicate somehow, their terror, their conquest of the urge to run and hide. Later, they would act as though they had deliberately carved their initials on a segment of history, a vicious history, but patriotic—and therefore rather noble, rather heroic.

In house-to-house fighting, we could glory in the windows we had broken; we had gone into homes, announced only by our explosive clatter, taking whatever we wished. We took food, trinkets, souvenirs, in a moment of wild optimism, acting out a crude script, after which, we were sure, we would go home unscathed and tell exciting stories about the war, as though it was a child's game and the bang-bang-bangs were all in fun. After all, we were among the dead, but not of them, not yet.

The happenstance of survival gave a special gloss to life, no matter how temporary it might be. Survivors seemed to feel that they were the privileged of the world. They acted as though they now knew there was no God, that there were no gods, only victorious men. Their language of survival made it clear that they felt brave, unvanquished, significant, historical even and that God could be quite wonderful, if cast in their image. And they had nothing but contempt for those who lagged behind, who sought cover as others leaped forward. Cowardly? Of course. How does one balance the will to survive against the folly of going forward? Prudence and logic are clearly on the side of *not* going forward, but then, there is emotion stretched to that neurotic degree called duty. It is for human beings the knowing submission to insanity. It is the smell of flesh burning, spilled brains, and the end of the world for those whose bodies we leave behind. And later, there are the troubling inner visions when you see yourself as you really are. You wrestle desperately with the fictitious image you wish the others to see; you compel yourself to do what any other beast will do, when running and hiding is impossible. You strike out blindly. That is war, the cold, noisy, abstruse and confused rude science. War deals with men, but not humanity.

The war would never be over, I used to think; only life would end. But, suddenly, one sun shiny day, in a tiny town in the Sudetenland, we heard the shouts that it was all over. "The war is over!" villagers shouted in German. Our men shouted it in English. Some screamed, "Shit! It's over." Others said they didn't believe it. But the sun was shining. It was a lovely day in May. I looked at the village. It had a small stone bridge over a little stream. Ducks swam in leisurely fashion. A woman swept cattle dung from the street, performing a duty that no war can interrupt. The place resembled a park. The houses were intact. There were no dead bodies, no litter—only this isolated place, as though there had never been any war at all. I wondered how all the threat and noise had disappeared so suddenly.

I wondered, too, what it all meant, or could mean. The history having been made, its interpreted meaning must now await the historians and what they tell us and what the children will study.

I can laugh now at the first time I was wounded. I did not know I had been hit. I felt nothing until somebody yelled, "Bruce, you're bleeding." I had no idea where, so my body became a solid blob of pain, as though I was anxious to make certain that I would hurt in the right place. It was in the hedgerow country, where I had felt safe because I could hide. I sat in the sun as it all came back to me, that summer of 1944. It was one trenchant and stinking tenant in the memory of my nose. The apple orchards had been brutalized by artillery. Apples and the bodies of cows rotted in the heat. Bees and flies were everywhere. The flies were moving in dark clouds as they scavenged. The cows that were alive seemed stunned, uncertain, as they browsed. Sweat, cow dung, blood, death, and noise announced their harsh competition. In the midst of it all, French farmers seemed like wound-up robots, stoics; some farm women were seen trampling huge vats of rotten apples, making that paralyzing potion known as Calvados. One gulp helped all of us move forward with sedated fear, resigned but not immune, slogging through the apple slush, the dung, and past the bodies, some of whom we used to know.

That day the medics picked me up, cut off my backpack and lashed me to a stretcher placed across the hood of a Jeep. I asked for my notebook in the pack and my Lifetime Schaeffer fountain pen. I forgot to ask for ink. It occurred to me that in the land of Descartes, Proust, and Ravel, surely there would be ink.

At the battalion surgeon's tent, I was washed and inspected, tested for broken bones. Finally, I was told that I had a "million dollar" wound, one that was flesh only, one that would heal and allow me, after a rest, to rejoin my regiment. In the hospital, I wrote my impression of the war. I remembered Father Flynn, an Army chaplain back in the States, whose addiction to the bottle was as strong as his losing battle with temptation. He was another Oscar Wilde dramatizing that he could resist "anything except temptation." He had made many predictions about the war. "We are all victims of civilization," he would say, especially when he had been drinking. "It'll be one hell of a scene, when Christ has His Second Coming. It might be advisable for him to put it off for a bit. If He comes as a pacifist, He will be suspect and ridiculed." I listened. I was still at Fort Dix at that time, playing tennis and spending weekends in New York. "If he comes during the War," Father Flynn went on, "He'll have to learn how to walk on blood, with spirited music by an American Legion band. Then what happens? Well, we'll have death everlasting; forget life. The world is so deeply mired in feces, that the most useful role for the humility of Christ will be as a wiper of the world's sphincter. He might also find it useful to learn how to walk on shit." He was drunk again. I was shocked, hearing what seemed to me to be heresy. Perhaps his alcohol was truth serum. But I was stunned to hear this man, so precise in his celebration of the Eucharist and the other rituals of his calling. It was Father Flynn I thought of when I wrote that there is no theological plumbing that can stop the leak in the seminal pipes, or the seminary ones. But at the time of my bleeding, he was far away. My wound made me believe, for a wild moment, that the war was over for me, although I had been told that there were no fractures and that I would be back with my unit in couple of weeks. The young heal quickly and I was sent back to duty. But I had no idea of any of this at the time I wrote what I rather pompously called

MILLENNIUM:

gather all
the nervous
pieces
twitching ganglia
and gore;
medicate
the melancholy—
there is
nothing more

I must have been under the influence of e. e. cummings in those days.

I rejoined the 26th Regiment as it headed for the Elbe and Germany. There, I won my second commendation for rescuing a white soldier who had rashly exposed himself and yelled, "I'm hit!" as he tumbled down the embankment into the roadway we were defending. Artillery whistled over our heads, towards the rear. A machine gun peppered the side of the embankment.

Since the bullets never went below a certain point, I assumed that I could crawl under them to reach the soldier in the roadway. I took off my pack and wiggled my way towards him. He demanded water, a demand that, as an ex-medic, I refused. He had been hit in the stomach. There was a small hole in his shirt and very little blood. I placed my hands beneath his back so that I could wiggle my way back. I almost vomited. My hands sank into a bloody mess. The bullet or bullets had torn him open.

We got back to the main line, just fifteen feet away. The slow wiggle lasted, it seemed, for hours. I was drowning in my own sweat. The soldier was mumbling about dying and God and making promises never to be unfaithful to his wife or to hit her again. Despite the awkwardness of the moment, he asked, over and over again, if I had a bible. I said nothing.

The real medics took over, and the soldier was taken away, strapped to the back of a Jeep. I never saw him again, although, indirectly, I learned of his fate. Some weeks after the incident, I was summoned to the company headquarters, where the captain shared with me a letter from the wounded soldier's wife. Responding to the word of her husband's death, she added at the bottom of her letter, "Thank the colored boy who tried to save my husband." The medal I received reminded me of my Aunt Catherine who had always prayed for my salvation to Saint Jude, the patron saint of hopeless causes. After all, I had not saved the soldier at all, but merely helped him go to a clean place to die.

Only two other episodes seem remarkable enough to mention. In Germany, while defending an airport from a German counterattack, we were stalled for three days. In a foxhole with me was a soldier from Chicago. We pored through our packs and reread old letters to pass the time. We ate K-Rations. Each ration container had a small slip of white paper bearing the legend, "Inspected By . . ." followed by a name. As one slip fluttered out, I caught a glimpse of some crude handwriting in pencil. I picked it up, as though it were great literature. It was good for a grim laugh, the kind that responds to something so unfunny that it is ridiculous. The inspection slip bore a female name. She had added in what Arthur Koestler has referred to as the neat and legible script of the illiterate, a morale building message: "Good luck, soldier. Write to me if you are white." She must have anticipated the possibility of integration and wanted to be certain that she would not receive a black soldier's letter.

Immediately, I wrote a steamy love letter to her, accompanied by a photograph of the blackest soldier I could find. He loved the idea. For some reason that had nothing to do with his color, he was known as "Red." Red had two teeth missing in the front and a hairdo that would later come to be known as an Afro. His was as wild and untamed as the kind of coiffure that Don King would make famous. His helmet could not depress his hair and always sat at what seemed to be an unbalanced angle. He had to add some string to the strap in order to tie it beneath his chin. I enclosed his grinning snapshot in my letter. The company's lieutenant and I had become friends of a sort. His roommate at the University of New Hampshire had been a track star, and he and I had much to discuss. He allowed me to mail the letter since it had no military content. Until the end of the war, the lieutenant never failed to ask if I had heard from the woman. Strangely, I never did. Neither did Red.

And then came that beautiful and shining day, near the border of the former Czechoslovakia, that the war ended. We were quickly assembled. I was part of a group sent to head-quarters to be a part of a memorial service for those who had died. White leggings were issued from somewhere and we were in what must have been the town square, dominated by a fountain and a small statute of Til Eulenspiegel, Germany's folklore scamp. How symbolic, I thought, that we should con-vene to mourn our war dead in the presence of a scamp. Somehow, to me, it seemed the perfect metaphor, the oxy-moron of war as meaningful, as thoughtful resolution of a dispute.

On the day the war ended in May, 1945, I celebrated the miracle of survival in a poem of recollection:

> I remember the tired tumult of my urges,
> and the sun shining, and the dust and the clouds,
> and how I turned my rifle down;
> I remember a cow stinking in the street
> and a woman calmly sweeping dung . . .
> I recall that hymns for the dead were sung,
> attention stood, and two colonels wept,
> but there was I,
> having dug holes in history,
> now stretched out alive
> on the same continent with Paris . . .

STILL IN UNIFORM, STILL IN TROUBLE

The First Infantry Division was to be assigned to duty at the war crimes trials in Nuremberg. We rejoiced that we would not be sent to the Pacific, where the war continued. We were told that new uniforms would be issued. However, the black soldiers would not be part of that well-dressed assignment. Suddenly, orders were issued transferring all of the black surviving volunteers to a new unit, called combat engineers—a fancy name for another kind of labor battalion. Many of us were furious, a feeling that was intensified when we reached the west coast of France, where these units were being redeployed for service in the Pacific, or for assignment in the States. Those who remained in France as "engineers," were told that we would be digging ditches where sewage lines would be laid. We would be working with Nazi prisoners of war. Hurriedly, I wrote a letter to Eisenhower, reminding him of his promise made in England, that we would never be segregated again, and protesting the unacceptable assignment to work alongside German prisoners.

The letter was then carried to Paris by my first scout, Albert Hartzog, who had by that time inserted a "von" before the Hartzog. "Hot Dog," as he was known, took a Jeep from the motor pool and sped on his way. He reported back that he had in fact left the letter at the headquarters in Paris. Naturally, we never had any response. I invited those who wished to protest the assignment to work with the German prisoners to join me just outside the camp's perimeter. Of the three hundred or so there, only thirty joined me. By that time, the commanding officer had sensed that a disturbance was at hand.

We did not know it at the time, but because of the racial over-tones and some of the more vulgar and explicit remarks of some of the soldiers about racism, and assertions that that was not what we had been fighting about, a peacemaker had been called. He was the aforementioned General Benjamin O. Davis, Sr. Two days after our demonstration, he appeared. I was summoned before him. He sat in a tent accompanied by a white lieutenant with a stenographer's pad. The lieutenant took down everything in shorthand. I felt sophisticated, despite my anger, when the General opened our talk by ask-ing, "Private Wright, haven't we met somewhere before, New York, London, Paris?" I had seen him only once before and that was at the Harlem YWCA at a 1942 dance, where I had gazed upon his presence in awe. His questions were gentle and peace-seeking. He did caution me about some of my remarks to the black soldiers, saying that it was suggested that I was inciting to riot, a very serious military offense. He urged me to think of my career as a law student and the con-sequences of a dishonorable discharge. He concluded the ses-sion by saying that I should go home and that I had been overseas long enough.

AWOL

Orders came almost immediately, transferring me to the States via troopship. At the port of embarkation, along with others, I mounted a gangplank to a much larger vessel than the one on which I had left New York. There was great confusion, crowding and much hilarity and joy among the men on their way home. I had on my Class A uniform, decorated with my combat infantryman's badge and medals, including a shoulder decoration awarded to the First Division itself that we were entitled to display. A naval officer, staring straight at me and focusing his gaze on my decorations, said, casually, to another officer, "I didn't know niggers were in combat." It was then that I knew that I did not wish to return to America. I did a right-about face that would have pleased a drill sergeant, and in the general confusion, simply walked off the ship with my duffel bag and the typewriter that I had looted from a German schoolhouse. I went to the nearby train station, bought a third-class ticket, and took a local to Paris.

In Paris, I went to the home of the famous Léopold Sédar Senghor, who had once professed a great interest in my poetry. He introduced me to Henri-Marcel Bernfeld, who put me up in a room in one of his father's apartments on the Boulevard de l'Obervatoire. Bernfeld, his father, and a brother had slept, at a different place almost every night of the German occupation of Paris, until hidden by a Roman Catholic priest who gave them the name, "Bennett." The father was a rather famous lawyer in Paris. He had represented refugees from fascist Spain without asking any payment. In return they had given him hundreds of gifts, all having something to do with Cervantes and *Don Quixote*. There were huge paintings, large and small sculptures, books of all sizes. Bernfeld's father had to rent a second apartment to house all of the gifts. I was installed in this apartment. I had met Senghor in 1944, shortly after the liberation of Paris. It was at the segregated or Negro Red Cross Club, near Pigalle. Cameron

Haynes, a former college classmate was in charge. Clever, debonair, and breezy, he asked if I was crazy in volunteering for the infantry, when the safe Red Cross was available. He seemed to forget that I had been drafted. Remembering that I had been class poet, he said, as though mentioning a casual afterthought, "There was some African guy in here earlier; just escaped from a German prisoner-of-war camp. He wanted to know if I knew any black American poets. He said he'd be back. He was weird and needed a haircut. He asked if I knew Langston Hughes. Maybe he'll come back." He did, that afternoon, and it was there that I met Léopold Sédar Senghor. He spoke no English and I very little French.

Senghor was hungry for news of Hughes, Gwendolyn Brooks, and Katherine Dunham. He said I must learn French and that English was harsh and teutonic. Senghor gave me small assignments at *Présence Africaine*, the magazine published by and for French speaking Africans and used by Senghor extensively to promote the theory of Négritude, a literary concept founded by Senghor, Léon Damas and Aimée Césaire. Damas was from French Guyana and Césaire from Martinique. Négritude seems an entirely mystical literary concept, an emphasis on Negro characteristics, both physical and cultural, in every aspect of life. It is a complex itch upon the soul. Indeed, Senghor cited Soul as the American counterpart of Négritude and praised Langston Hughes as its prophet in America. It was about such subjects that Senghor felt so passionately and with whom I often spoke, as though it was a duty that somehow paid for my flight from the United States Army and the refuge he offered to me. My father had jokingly said to me before I was drafted that if the Army sent me to Europe and I did not go to Paris, I was no son of his. Absent without leave, in Paris, I would often think of his joking admonition, the only sign of his humor that I remember.

I will always be grateful to Senghor for incredible seasons in Paris—even limited in its amenities—as I made my way about the city avoiding military police and any other sight of American or military authority. Paris, for me, with its on-and-off electricity failures, its elevators stranded between floors, remains a glorious memory. The architecture seemed pure poetry and I had read so much about the city that I wandered its streets amazed that it all seemed so familiar.

Among the souvenirs I was taking back to America, before I walked off the ship and came to Paris, were several books of passes, each pass good for two weeks. Using my looted typewriter, I managed to survive occasional stops by MPs. They saw the indecipherable scrawl signed above the line designated Commanding Officer, knew that no black wrote in such a sophisticated style, and I was never detained beyond such an inspection.

At the Théatre des Champs Élysées on the Avenue Montaigne on December 4th, that year of 1945, I attended a strange concert; not that the music was strange, but the circumstances. Rudolph Dunbar, a black American conducted a concert of American music. It was bitterly cold, as was the theater. Many of the members of the Orchestre de la Société des Concerts du Conservatoire wore gloves. Dunbar, formal in his allegiance to the dress code for such an occasion, wore tails, but he was such a physically active conductor that he was probably the only warm person in the auditorium. The music was disappointing in some ways, for as the program said it was a grand festival of American music. I had hoped to hear *Le Tombeau de Couperin,* my favorite Ravel composition and an homage to the dead. My attendance at the concert marked another time of refuge without detection. With my false passes, I had become brazen. It was a far cry from my second wound. When I lay for hours in the snow occasionally conscious, I had never lost my sophomoric sense of humor and I had sworn to those who looked to the heavens for divine armor, that if I thought I was dying, I'd make a joke with my last breath. I was then certain that the time had come. At one point I awoke to a familiar mumble "Sanctus Espirito." I saw a cross and looked into the face of a chaplain. I interrupted his last rites saying, "Father . . . if you don't get me out of here, *I* will be the last Wright." I had satisfied my desire to make even death a bad joke.

I spoke to Senghor about becoming a citizen of France and renouncing my American citizenship. It was dismaying to learn that I would have to go through the American embassy. As an AWOL, that course did not promise success.

Then the day came when I ran out of blank passes. Stopped by a zealous MP, my cheery greeting was ignored as he methodically consulted his alphabetical list of AWOLS. I was there, of course, and I was arrested on the spot and taken to a suburban detention stockade. There, I joined what seemed a virtual army of other delinquents. The commanding officer, new to his overseas service, had not seen combat and he was impressed by my medals and other decorations, including my combat infantry badge. He had no knowledge of a black presence in famous divisions and he questioned me closely. I regaled him with what I thought was a suitably modest recital of my adventures. He seemed impressed and said what a pity it was that so many soldiers who had fought and been wounded should be kept in the stockade. Finally, he promised that if I could get a German Luger for him, I would be restricted to barracks, instead of the prisonlike enclosure of the stockade. Getting a Luger was easy. Almost every soldier was bringing such souvenirs back to America, including ammunition. For the fifty francs it cost me, I delivered the Luger and was assigned to new quarters.

Shamelessly, in the evening, I walked away from the encampment and returned to Paris. After all, I had not made my goodbyes to Senghor and other merciful friends. I had sprouted a couple of hairs beneath my chin and I wanted to pick up my personal things, including a razor I had bought for my first shave. Again, I was arrested at Gare de l'Est. This time, there were no suburban amenities. Along with many others, I was linked together, blacks and whites in coerced integration, everyone an AWOL. We were herded onto a train and taken to Belgium. In Ostend, we were placed on various ships. I was placed on what seemed to be a freighter. It was not a troopship. Actually, I had a room and a shower. It was obviously the quarters of a minor officer.

The captain had been somehow associated with the First Infantry Division in World War I, and he and I talked before we sailed. He asked that I work on the ship's paper and be in close touch with the radio operator on a daily basis. The voyage would take several leisurely weeks, over what the captain called the southerly route, through waters thought to be relatively free of mines. In keeping with my fate as a ward of Saint Jude, my journalism career was a brief one. One day, the radio news was that a German officer, returning to the village of Nuenstein from his captivity, discovered that his wife had been having affairs with an American captain, a first lieutenant, and a second lieutenant. Apparently, all of them knew each other, and there were suggestions of group sex and other exotic expressions of passion. With teutonic thoroughness, the German killed all three officers. Obviously, he loved and forgave his wife, for he did not harm her. My headline that day for the paper was "Brass Polished Off." The ship's captain was furious. He upbraided me for joking, in effect, about the deaths of "some fine and patriotic officers who had fought for America." For the rest of the voyage, I simply loitered on the deck until we headed into the colder weather of the Atlantic. I had no idea what would happen to me as an AWOL. There was always the doubtful comfort of rumors, however, and they reported that the Army was glad to round up its AWOLS and get them back to the States. It was not quite that easy, however.

I was embarrassed. We put in at Bush Terminal in Brooklyn. Even for AWOLS, a military band played bravely as we disembarked, as though we were respectable returning warriors. Trucks took us to Fort Dix. There, a sergeant looking at my service record, exclaimed, "Wow! You were AWOL for a year and a half. That's desertion!" That had not occurred to me earlier, and to hear a very serious sergeant say that sent panic through my system. Immediately, I assumed my role as a first-year law school lawyer. I denied that I was absent for eighteen months, insisting that it was only eighteen days. I suggested that all records were in a mess during and after the war and that there must be some terrible mistake. "Listen," I said, "I'm a law student. I came back to complete law school and get on with my career." This, despite the fact that I had never wished to come back to America. I asked the sergeant to call my brother-in-law, who was at Fort Dix at the time I was drafted and was at the Separation Center when I returned. Apparently much respected at the post, my brother-in-law whispered a few minutes with the sergeant, and, after eighteen months of furtive liberation in Paris, I was officially docked eighteen-day's pay. It made little difference. In four years of military servitude, I had never had a furlough. With credit for that time, I received an honorable discharge and the $300 discharge stipend.

To mark my regard for a uniform that had been sullied by segregation, as soon as I arrived home, I threw it in the garbage. My medals and other awards, somehow missed the garbage. After my first two sons were born, they surfaced as toys for them. The decorations subsequently disappeared completely, along with my interest in the military, except to make certain that my sons, eligible for the carnage of Vietnam, served in the Peace Corps during that time of mistaken American chutzpah and murderous pride.

AFTER THE WAR, NOT-SO-FREE ASSOCIATIONS

The military experience had been a strange one for me. I had always resisted discipline, but had never had even a modest triumph when its power was brought to bear upon me. Almost without exception, the question of religious morals had arisen, with the warning of rewards for moral behavior and penalties for the opposite. I had always had a lawyer's desire, I suppose, for evidence and I could discover none that justified an unquestioning belief in what I regarded as sectarian fictions and devotion to some great bearded shape in a white Protestant heaven. In combat, the most desperate of crises, God is always invoked by soldiers. To encourage such superstition, chaplains are much in evidence and there are always rumors of miracles and occurrences that have no relationship with common sense or reason.

Thousands can still rally in some urban or rural place with their faithful fears and belief, waiting to bear witness to a statue weeping, or anxious to see the face of Christ upon a piece of cloth. Everyone, it seems, has a god of one kind or another. There is Mr. Goodwrench, immaculate in spotless overalls, assuring America in perfect syntax of his infallibility as a pope of mechanical mystery. Obviously, he is relying on the American addiction to faith, anti-intellectualism, its spiritual business. Millionaire evangelists and missionaries and television *nuncios* rule the Sunday airwaves, as though they are personal secretaries to the God they so enthusiastically advertise. Separation of church and state becomes a fiction as Billy Graham visits the White House, while a chaplain blesses Congress.

As video clergymen become trusted symbols of family values and fiscal virtue, one can doubt that they make money in an old-fashioned way. They are as agile in their insider dealing with God as the wealthy arbitrageurs and junk-bond sovereigns are in their pursuit of the dollar's manifest destiny. They are with us in every war and God, the Great Mugwump, is on everyone's side.

I did not know it at the time I left the army, but Bill Cosby was to become a national avuncular symbol, almost a rival of Uncle Sam in attracting the nation's affection. As Dr. Huxtable, he was the dark centerpiece of nonthreatening black bourgeoisie comfort. His smile dazzled and became an instant placebo easing thoughts of black struggle and its vulgar ordeal. Cosby, it seemed, could buy a house anywhere, without fear of a cross-burning or the objections of neighbors.

At the war's end, I became lawless and heedless of consequences that I knew could be dire, although I feared daily being caught before I had had my surfeit of Paris. I fell in love with Paris, the city, the streets, the scenes and the history itself. I felt genuinely free. America in 1945 was still practicing its popular Christian sport of lynching blacks. I had been wrong about the benefits of blacks volunteering for combat as a way to make things better racially. Eisenhower had broken his promise that if we volunteered, we would never be segregated again. It had been ridiculous, anyway, for America, as a shining knight, to save the free world from the predatory racism of the Nazis while at the same time having a racially segregated army. Hypocrisy was raised to the level of a canon when America's generals opposed integration yet Eisenhower led the country's brotherhood movement.

It is true that the Army brought me back to America, but it is equally true that I never truly returned. Quite apart from the charismatic and Pentecostal movements, America has always nourished an anti-intellectual energy. But, as I was assured, things were never as bad as they seemed. After all, James Earl Jones was to become a national spokesman for a telephone company that at one time would not employ a black. But white South Africans continued to suppress the black majority there, while the Dutch trespassers continued their pious worship in the Dutch Reformed Church. Those who preferred the Church of England were little better. The period immediately after the war was, I thought, the same mixture as before. Clearly, the black circumstance was not something pressing upon the American mind and the nation's attention could be focused on the blacks—not the black circumstance—through destructive riots. Military supremacy would become the sought objective and ideal. Eventually, the army would join in the seduction of the young and like a Pied Piper, the young would be told to be all that they could be, by joining the army.

In Louisiana, one Susie Phipps discovered that some-where along the genetic line, she had a black forebear. She sued to have her racial classification changed from black to white. She envisioned a better life on earth, at least, if her lineage could be officially laundered and bleached by the detergent of a bureaucratic document.

What did remain the same after the Good War was the country's feeling for God as a white Protestant Christian. And once, each December, Jesus Christ, born a Jew and then a rabbi, became America's bestselling fiction, a crucial fiction, so to speak. It was a pardonable offense to drink too much in this passing time of good feeling. This was precisely the kind of America to which I had no wish to return, but did.

I was to witness an eruption of surface definitions. Negroes were no longer to be called Negroes, but black, a color that most are not. Now, some years later, they were to move on into a kind of alien nationalism and to be told by their leaders that they were African–Americans. Except for their indelible inheritance of melanin, of course, black is the last thing they are. To justify such a designation as no longer a fighting adjective, it had to be believed that there was some mystical power to the new hyphenated status, such as Irish-American. It was as though being called African–Americans would somehow give blacks a country. European–Americans, however, are very different. They have a clearly identifiable homeland, or that of their ancestors. Most African–Americans know little about Africa and virtually nothing about their tribal or village origins, or even what country in Africa their ancestors knew. Family origins have not only been diluted, they have been wiped out. English names now substitute for those of antiquity, bloodlines have been diluted, and the only constant remaining is color.

Alex Haley invented some arresting fictions that made him well-to-do and aided the reputations of some black actors, but did little for the truth. That Haley had plagiarized some writings of a white author dashed the hopes of those who wanted to believe in a touchable national kinship with the kings, princes, and chiefs of Africa and bloodlines that connected them with a nation. It was all wasted passion and a history reluctant to reveal identities. We remain immigrant aliens in America, as we have been since the earliest importations to the Americas and the West Indies. Nevertheless, the black gene remains afflicted with an incurable ache, a melancholy and nameless longing for a vague and lost ancestral linkage. In our miscegenetic discontent, many speak of going "home" again, to a place to which it is far too late to have, which we cannot know and probably would not love if we did "return," except as tourists or curious travelers. All genetic linkage has been aborted other than our color.

And yet, we dream. It is our artificial respiration and is as unreal as our dark imitation of white life. We who bear the scarred beauty of black, treasure small comforts, no matter how transient. We are dreamers; we nurture illusions and search for non-menace. We try to believe we are quintessential Americans, second only to the Indians, who have been evicted and banished by their invading landlord. Once rulers of America's incredible geography, the former indigenous peoples have become indigent tenants, displaced persons. They, too dream of their ancient nations and of avenging Wounded Knee. They cherish fitful visions as they huddle in their assigned and always shrinking reservations. And now, they, too, are becoming Americans in quest of fiscal rainbows, as they seek the therapy of money machines in their casinos. They seek to shape profitable oases in their otherwise mean deserts.

Black Americans remain different from other immigrants. We do not speak the languages of our forefathers. At one time, our ancestors were the only immigrants to America who could never receive a letter or a package from home. They could not even drop a card back to the old tribe, saying, "Glad you're not here." They did not even know where "here" was, and, in any event, it was a crime for them to learn to read or write. If we look "homeward" to Africa, it can be with no genuine nostalgic speed-up of the pulse, but with the wonderment of divorce from what we never knew. And so, in some desperation, we cling to America and the West Indies with the pathetic tension of a people without a country, cut off from tribal memories. Most have now become students of pious biblical servitude, adopting the religion of the slaveowners.

An expatriate census without a patria, we inhabit a

world of intimate strangers. Wearing the blemish of our pigmentation, we are, in effect, citizens without a country, a theme and variation on the argosy of Philip Nolan. Visionaries and illusionists, we have given energy to survival by permitting images of desire to feed upon each other. Many whites, joyous in their pale privilege, marvel at bitter blacks and perceive in them an ingratitude for democracy's blessings, of which, some believe, slavery was one. Roger Brooke Taney screams at us from the grave that he told us so when he wrote in his Dred Scott decision that African imports were never intended to become citizens of the United States.

My visits to the slave ports of West Africa extracted tears for those unknown ancestors who suffered their kidnapped voyage across the infamous Middle Passage. I looked into the many faces that so closely resembled my father; I saw evidence of my paternal origins. I thought, too, about the ten million or so unmarked tidal graves of the Africans at the bottom of the sea, the drowned ghosts, once solid flesh. I touched the iron manacles in the walls of the slave dungeons and tried to summon some passion for unknown tribes, unknown relatives, but I could place no genetic mortgage on time, place, or person. But African kinship has continued to keep a doubtful rhythm in my emotions as my heartbeat sometimes stutters out of time. And, with a sense of inexplicable shame, I know I can never be an African. The dilution has been too thorough. In any event, I've convinced myself that, with so many miscellaneous genes, it is impossible to select among them for some identification with the past, some blood loyalty, some special sin of pride.

I did not come from a family of writers. No one in my

family kept a diary that I was aware of. . . . The longest letter I ever received from my father was when I was in college. Each semester, it was the same, in his labored handwriting. He would enclose a money order for $3 and say: "Dear Son, hear is some money for you. Study hard, love, Daddy." That was it. Recalling it today exacts a tear, for it was the middle of the Great Depression and I knew it was not easy for him.

In a time of great unemployment, my father always managed to have two or three jobs at the same time. A baker by trade, he was also, sometimes, a cook and a gas station attendant. Asthma made him wheeze and rheumatism made him limp. The asthma was worse than anything else. Often, he would sink down in a chair and light some vile smelling powder, inhaling and gasping at the same time. The stink of that powder clings to my nose to this day, almost half a century after his death. I never heard him complain about his condition. He seemed to accept it as just something that he had. Now and then, he would say something disparaging about his height, all of five feet four inches. Despite his quiet temperament, he must have had a rather large ego, for he married my mother, a white woman almost a head taller than he. He was fifty-six when he died of another torture added to his life of affliction: cancer. Gray and wizened by 1946 when I was discharged from the army, he was often hospitalized. It was difficult for me to talk with him and see his obvious suffering. Healthy and impatient with illness, I was embarrassed when he said I looked well and he told me to take care of myself. He was proud that all three of his children had gone to college and he seemed reconciled to my failure to become a doctor. In our last visit, he asked when I would become a lawyer, not if. He wanted something to relish in advance, something to brag about at his barber shop, His last words to me as we parted, were, "Son, the next time you see me, I'll be. . . ." He stopped, as though not to mention death would prevent it. He always called me "Son," never Bruce. A week after that visit, he died—free at long last, of his aches and pains.

My brother, sturdy and quiet and close to my grandfather, as though he was preparing to be one himself, was devoted to my father and looked after him tenderly. Even as I could never realize my father's ambition for me to become a doctor, neither could I ever help with that bag that had been surgically attached to one of my father's intestines. My brother, who was much closer to nature and its rude insults than I, is the one who should have been a doctor. I never knew his ambitions, except for his desire after World War II to have a mink farm. For a while, he did realize that ambition and he had a thriving mink farm in New Jersey. Eventually, his wife objected to the odor of the animals and protested that he would have to choose between her and his minks. By that time, everyone in the family had something made of mink fur. Wounded and deprived, he became a milkman.

No one in New Jersey had ever seen a black milkman before. He was an undemonstrative first. He was not talkative and never had been. He worked hard at whatever he did and he became manager of the dairy where he worked. Earlier, for a time, we were at Lincoln University together, although he roomed with someone else. I knew nothing about his studies at Lincoln. We both played football. He was tall and well-built, after my mother's side of the family. Gentle and deliberate, he was strong. He played football reluctantly, but much better than I. Our small and all-male university in rural

Pennsylvania had a famous football coach. In fact, there were two. Manuel Rivero was known as the Mad Cuban. He had distinguished himself on the Columbia team that upset Stanford and won at the Rose Bowl sometime in the thirties. Jerome Holland, the other coach, had been an All-American at Cornell. Often, there were not enough football players to have a scrimmage with eleven players on each side. If a student weighed over one hundred pounds, he was expected to play or at least try out for the team. At 185 pounds, I could not escape. Reluctant or not, my brother excelled. The coaches knew that my play was unpredictable. It was my only distinction on the field. On the one occasion when the press thought my play was worthy of notice, I was called "Bruce White."

The only other time my play was thought worthy of comment was after the war in Europe, when the regiment fielded a team. The regimental newspaper commenting upon the team's win, said "Captain Bruce Wright played a bang-up game." I was still a private, but, inexplicably, I had been elected team captain. I sent the clipping to my mother and she noised her pride around the neighborhood and the arsenal, where she operated a forklift. She was visibly shocked when I appeared as a private.

Despite family photo albums, in my youth I could never picture my parents or Aunt Catherine as ever having been young; nor did it occur to me that my teachers had ever been young. Early along, I determined that any children I might have would be able to consult a record of my youth and that time before they were born. Looking at photos of me as a child, and even as a college student, they ask, "Who is that?"

I have been much less than thorough in my biographical

recordkeeping. Except for a few letters to *The New York Times* railing about that paper's failure to send late editions to Harlem, I never kept copies of my writings to mistresses, wives, children, or parents and others. A family member who was distant from family, but always needed one, I have had several with my five marriages. Despite those Hollywoodlike numbers, I have counted only three that had any promise of success, and that was because I believe three really loved me and I have cherished them, after my adulterous fashion. One mother-in-law I really loved. My fifth wife believes me to be incapable of love. As she is not a psychoanalyst to whom I have made confessions, I am deeply offended by her lay analysis. Perhaps that is because it may be closer to the truth than I like. I have been called a womanizer by close friends, both male and female. While I have been intrigued by many women, I have never been arrogant enough to believe that I ever pleased them, in bed or out, except, perhaps, when I washed the dishes.

An autobiography, then, especially at the age of 76, becomes a jumbled and haphazard diary of afterthoughts, an impossible attempt to bridge distances from feeling and past-tense reality. But, as Catherine Drinker Bowen put it in the parsing of her own life, "Before one can know that the elders too have been young and vulnerable, one must be old one-self." Unlike Ms. Bowen, I have no records to footnote memory, no packets of family letters, no copies of daily jottings and no historical reach-back to long ago. It is as though I stem from a tradition of mutes and autistic ancestors. I did think it rather remarkable that my grandfather had been born in 1857, the historical significance of which, I believe he knew nothing, although he read the *Daily Graphic* and the *Sun* studiously. I remember, once, in passing, he spoke of his own grandfather. That would have reached back to the 1700s. My maternal grandmother was a year older than her husband. Of her thirteen children, my mother was next to the youngest. My father's family remains a mystery. I did hear that his father's name was John. I have no recollection of his mother or her name. The substance of an autobiography, as with a biography or any other writing, however, is as important because of what is put in or left out. These dredgings from untrustworthy memory shape as nearly as benevolent treachery allows, whatever I am now, whatever I believed I wanted to be and whatever I sought to be.

GULLIBLE'S TRAVAILS

In Which I am Exposed to the Rude Reality of What Charles Mingus Has Titled

Life Beneath The Underdog

In 1951, I began a series of intellectual adventures in the classes of Professor Horace M. Kallen at the New School. At the same time, I was embarking upon another kind of experience, the visceral one of getting to know jazz musicians, their language, their music, and the ordeals that defined their lives and deaths and their hells in between. I sought to assuage my sensitivities by remembering quotations from Cyril Connolly's *The Unquiet Grave*, the melancholy essays that enthralled my college sophomore discoveries. Especially as I got to know the jazz scene and saw how so many of the performers inadvertently committed suicide through joyous overindulgence and the compulsion of chemical overdoses.

To recall and write about these experiences, some have said, is to write about the lives of others, instead of my own. But, the lives of black musicians traveling the world as messengers of their art presented a memorable pageant for me and, I believe, had much to do with the kind of person I became and the kind of judge I became in assessing conflicts and reaching decisions about the human circumstance and especially the sickness of addiction and its often deadly side-effects. The insights uttered by some of the musicians have remained indelibly in my mind and have become a part of me. They left impressions that became an inseparable part of my thought processes on the bench and off. Many people remember the public fits of temper displayed by Charles Mingus from one bad gig or another, and many were surprised to read his in-depth anger in his book *Beneath the Underdog*. It was the in-depth stoicism, as well, that was a kind of perverse example of Cyril Connolly's thought that there should be no disappointment, because there is no appointment in life. If so, that is a sufficient reason for the genius of improvisation in the music that some call jazz but the improvisers call simply music, *their* music.

For one, such as myself, weaned on the violin for eight years of hated lessons, jazz became a very special expression of music, of life, anger, reached-for serenity, and the same heartbreak as the Negro spiritual. It was James Baldwin who said somewhere that until some devastating white experience of spiritual trauma occurred, no white would ever compose the kind of psychological devastation represented by a song such as "Sometimes I Feel Like A Motherless Child." Jazz has that kind of anguish, too. Aldous Huxley in *Crome Yellow* addressed its hypnotic contagion: "David did not dance—but when ragtime came squirting out of the pianola in gushes of treacle and hot perfume, in jets of Bengal light, then things began to dance inside him. Little black nigger corpuscles jigged and drummed in his arteries. He became a cage of movement, a walking *palais de danse.*" Huxley's use of the term "little black nigger" did more to define his limitations than it did to define jazz.

My experiences with musicians came about in a rather round-about way. I had done some complex legal work for a family called Bates—work that would make a book in itself. There were four daughters in the family, three still alive.

One of them, Susan, then in her teens, came down with me to Greenwich Village to the Cafe Bohemia. Art Blakey and the Jazz Messengers were playing, delivering their message of hard bop to the sophisticates who venerated the latest quirks in life and its nighttime diversions. I had never heard of Art Blakey at the time, although, along with Max Roach, Blakey was regarded as one of the greatest jazz drummers in the world. He had changed his name to Abdullah Buhaina when he became a Muslim. Susan was captivated by him. Eventually, she and Blakey planned to be married. By that time I had gotten to know Art and told him that he shouldn't get married since he was then undivorced from his first wife. Art's reply was both true and wholly unrealistic: "Well, I've never been married under my Muslim name before." That was but a short time after they had been dating. Before their marriage, Susan told me that Art really needed legal advice. She suspected that he was being cheated by producers, and underpaid—a condition I was later to discover was charac-

Me in 1921.

My parents, Louise and Bruce Wright.

A study in sartorial
elegance, the Wright
siblings in 1926.
From left, Bruce McM.,
Nita, and Robert.

Lincoln University, November 1941. I may have looked tough, but I only made the scrub team.

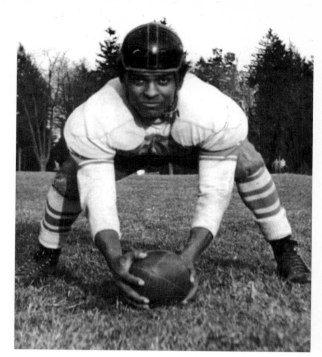

My senior year high-school picture.

Having survived World War II, this picture was taken in 1945 when I went AWOL in Paris.

In this 1942 oil portrait of me, artist Keith Simon wanted to give a face to black men's feelings towards racism.

In 1951 my mother and I were visiting Washington, D. C., when I spotted this sign. "You have to take a picture of this," I said. Just then, a policeman—in those days, he was, of course, white—came up to us.
"Is this boy . . . ," indicating me, " . . . bothering you?"
"Oh," my mother replied, "he's been bothering me for twenty-eight years."

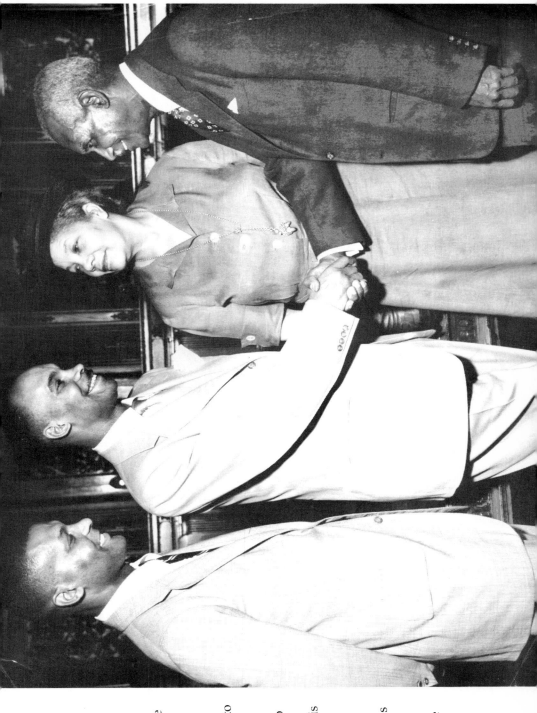

June 29, 1951, on the occasion of James L. Watson's admission to the New York Bar. From left to right, me, James L., his mother Violet, and his father, Judge James S. Watson, the first black judge in New York's history.

With perhaps somewhat inflated expectations, in 1950, I opened my first law office at Fifth Avenue and Forty-third Street. On the bookshelf, above my head, is a picture of Thurgood Marshall, who was to become the first black justice of the United States Supreme Court.

Having dinner at my West 107th Street apartment in 1965 with Fernando Howard (left), my former law partner, and President Léopold Sédar Senghor of Sénégal.

At my swearing-in, flanked by one of my mentors, prominent civil rights attorney Hope Stevens (left) and my oldest son, Geoff (the one with the hair).

Being sworn in as judge of the Criminal Court, February 1970, by Mayor John V. Lindsay.

I was very much opposed to the war in Vietnam and wore that peace button even on my judicial robes, much to the consternation of the administrative judge. I was not going to sacrifice my sons to that misguided, unconscionable effort, so I called in a lot of favors to get them into the Peace Corps.

PHOTO CREDIT: *Kwame Brathwaite*

After my shocking victory in the 1979 campaign for Civil Court.

PHOTO CREDIT: *Kwame Brathwaite*

Opposite: During the campaign for New York Supreme Court in
1982, the candidate demonstrating graceful restraint.

PHOTO CREDIT: *Charmian Reading*

My mother Louise on a 1968 visit to Buffalo, New York. She's buried in the white section of a Princeton cemetery, my father in the black.

In the U.S. Virgin Islands, 1974, with my brother-in-law, Dr. James A. Moss.

Finishing the Harlem 10k footrace of 1992 in under an hour. Son Keith (he's number 376) trailed me in case I had a heart attack.

With another survivor of the Harlem 10K, Roscoe Brown, president of the Bronx Community College.

With Max Roach, the renowned jazz drummer, at the Paul Robeson Scholarship Benefit held at the United Nations on May 11, 1993. The Paul Robeson Scholarship in Minority Legal Studies was established in 1977 to perpetuate the ideals of social justice.

In front of New York's City Hall with council member C. Virginia Field, Governor Mario Cuomo, and my son the politician, Assemblyman Keith Wright. It was 1993, and we didn't have a clue that Cuomo would lose to George Pataki only a year later.

PHOTO CREDIT: *Karl Crutchfield*

The Wright brothers. Seated on the couch, sons Keith (holding his son Jared), Alexis, Patrick (the little guy on Alexis's lap), and oldest son Geoff. On the floor, Keith's wife Susan, son Bruce C.T., and me.

PHOTO CREDIT: *Patricia A.F. Wright*

Below: At home, on West 135th Street, with wife Patricia in 1982.

teristic of what was occurring in the professional lives of black jazz musicians.

When I first met Blakey, I was extremely uncomfortable. It was at a nightclub where he was performing. I went early to speak to him before performance time at 10 P.M. — my usual bed time. The world of jazz was a mystery to me. I knew of the big bands, of course, such as those of Cab Calloway, Duke Ellington, and Count Basie. Almost totally unknown to me were the jazz quartets and quintets, those musical adventurers who experimented in forms of improvisational expression known as hard bop. It was then that I became acquainted with Blakey's total disregard for punctuality, a practice he regarded contemptuously as a failing of naifs. As a lawyer, it was amazing to me that someone could be so cavalier about contracts affecting his livelihood. I had had eight years of violin lessons and knew about strict compliance with the demands of my instruction and the absolute importance of my one-hour allotment of practice time.

Blakey's philosophy then was that the public would wait for his genius and be rewarded by his playing overtime. When he finally appeared, he was high, drunk, I thought. Later I was to learn it was heroin.

"No, man, I don't need no lawyer," he said. "All I need is some gigs." I was appalled. I looked at Susan. She spoke to Art. I heard him say, "Okay, if he needs a little business, I'll let him look over my next contract, but Jack don't like lawyers." He was speaking of his manager, Jack Whittemore; and, as I was later to learn, Jack certainly did not care for lawyers. I assumed after meeting Art that I'd never be hearing from him again. When I did, it had nothing to do with music. He wanted to know how to get a marriage license in New York for him and Susan. I reminded him of his existing marriage. He said he believed his long separation from his first wife had ripened automatically into a divorce. Anyway, he said, "we were just kids and that was in Pittsburgh" his home town. I assured him that long separations did not become divorces in New York. He then repeated that he had never been married under his Muslim name. He added, as though that settled the matter, "Divorce is Christian and ain't got nothing to do with Islam."

In keeping with what was to become largely his practice when I became his lawyer, he ignored my advice and married Susan anyway. I outlined for him the probable legal consequences of the marriage if Susan ever learned the truth. He seemed unconcerned about bigamy. Eventually, they had two children and Art provided cash for Susan and her sisters to build a house on some vacant Vermont land they had inherited. According to Art, Susan wanted a home built of California redwood. And, he added, "If she wants it built of marble, she can have it." This seemed a bit improbable at the time, as Art was then being booked through Shaw Artists and Jack Whittemore at a weekly pay of twelve hundred dollars and sometimes even less. From that, he had to pay his four other musicians, pay for transportation, pay for a hotel and food. At the outset, agency commission was taken. I often wondered how he could afford heroin. I was to learn how later.

By the time of the marriage, Blakey's first wife had sued for support. On behalf of Blakey, I counterclaimed for divorce. Between depositions and other preparations for trial, Blakey was well aware that his version of Islamic belief and New York law were expensively incompatible. Blakey had one son at that time, Art Blakey, Jr., and two daughters by his first wife, then living in Brooklyn.

Blakey was a musical marvel who, it was said, did not know a note of music. He had achieved his great reputation through the genius of his instinct. Promoters and record companies realized his greatness and so did he, although he bewailed constantly how unfair it was that white musicians should be paid so much more handsomely than blacks. He had no complaint about Alfred Lion and Francis Wolf, the two immigrants from Germany who founded the Blue Note jazz label in the 1930s. They treated Art with the great respect they believed an inventive and creative artist should have. Prior to recording sessions, they would give Blakey enormous cash advances against royalties. Royalties for jazz recordings were always fairly minuscule and Art's never equalled his advances. The sales of so-called hit records were numbered in the thousands—not millions. The Modern Jazz Quartet was an exception, perhaps because their music was more disciplined than Bebop. Its members enjoyed an excellent business reputation and only one of its members was ever known to have been a heroin addict. Art liked the fact that Lion had married a black woman, although Art himself seemed to prefer others. He also preferred to forget his first wife. He had married her at fifteen or sixteen in their old Pittsburgh neighborhood, and they were parents by seventeen. Susan was an exception, of course. He never regarded her as half-black, but always as half-white.

When Susan wanted a house built, Blue Note advanced thousands of dollars. I have personally transported several twenty-thousand-dollars cash payments in cash to Vermont as the house progressed. Once, I drove Art's big Cadillac from New York to Vermont, with my briefcase bulging with cash.

The house was always in Susan's name. I advised Art to arrange to have his name on the deed as what the law calls a tenancy by the entireties, giving him an undivided one-half interest in the house. "It's Susan's house. Don't bug me about it." It was indeed Susan's house, as Art would soon discover to his dismay.

Art always wanted a home of his own, something that would symbolize an escape from the humble slum scenes of black Pittsburgh, a place over which he could preside as head of the family, a place where he could proudly have his friends and gather his children. Looking at his youth, it could not have been predicted that one day, he would be the heroin-addicted leader of a hard bop jazz group, playing marginal night clubs, being celebrated as *the* percussionist who transformed African drumming into what some writers and critics called an art form. And the more he traveled, the more he always wanted to return to a place he could call his own, *his* home. At twelve, he had been part of a family gospel group that sang hymns on Pittsburgh corners for whatever passersby would contribute in coins. Art played a tambourine, as his first "drum." This was the beginning of the folksy blues motif that would flavor all of his rhythmic playing and give each of his groups a special Blakey sound, a jazz-gospel continuity that would identify his music.

In his later jazz life, when he had moved indoors to the bars and clubs, he never mentioned his Evangelical, charismatic, and emotional religious childhood. The children of his first marriage remembered though. Gwen, the oldest of his first four children, recalled those days. So did Evelyn. Art, Jr. was perhaps too young to remember. Blakey was already building his jazz legend by the time Art, Jr. was born. He would become part of the history of Pittsburgh's treasure-trove of jazz greats. In his early days, Art gave no clue that drums would be central to his career. He preferred the piano and, as a teenager, thought of himself as a pianist. Indeed, when the pianist at Pittsburgh's Crawford Grill became ill, Art was installed as his substitute. But when the regular pianist returned, Art was out. He had been substituting for Erroll Garner, who would go on to be a prosperous celebrity of his own. Determined to be no undercard replacement, Art transferred his energy and feel for music, to the drums.

Blakey's daughter, Gwen, wanted me to write a biography of Art. He promised to cooperate. Gwen held a very responsible job with a Wall Street bond house and in good weather, she would walk up to my Foley Square chambers in the Supreme Court and chat about her recollections of Art's gospel life as a Christian troubadour and sidewalk performer of religious music. And even as he brought so much passion to his music, he brought that same quality to his life, his divorce from Christianity and his commitment to Islam. Gwen had amassed considerable material about her father, had traveled to Pittsburgh and to relatives in Ohio and other places to round up family members and photographs for her biography of her father. My own recollections of Art are no more than vignettes. He was in his early thirties by the time I met him and already recognized as a great performer. Gwen's researches were the real ingredients of a life. Perhaps whoever has her materials will write Art's true biography. It will be Gwen's book no matter who does it. In all of my chats with Gwen, she never complained about her health, even though she knew her cancer was spreading. It ultimately killed her, of course.

Gwen Blakey lived long enough to give her Muslim

father an emotional Christian funeral, with an elaborate coffin—everything that Art said he did not want when he was beyond wanting. His later children bore Japanese and Muslim names and there were benevolent disputes about the kind of funeral he would have. He had dictated to me his wish to have his remains disposed of quickly, after the Muslim fashion, but he was too sick to sign his will. At a time when he knew death was near, he and I sat for the photographer Eleana Steinberg's cameras and reminisced for several hours about the excitements and adventures we had shared in travels around the world. Perhaps she will do something for Gwen's uncompleted work. But then, she must first recover from her own grief. Shortly after I performed her marriage to Richard Tee, he became a victim of prostate cancer, lapsed into a semi-coma and died several months later.

Art had many loves, but he compared them all with Susan. He sacrificed much for her, her whims and demands. She remained central to his life and came from California to be near during the illness from which he died. He sought desperately to avoid death. There were sessions with acupuncture needles. There were the Japanese mystics who rolled him from his apartment in his wheelchair to secret devotions and ministrations. There were the doctors from St. Vincent's and there were the Christian believers, who simply prayed. I never saw an official from a mosque. Art's funeral was a contest between his Christian and Muslim survivors. The Muslims wanted the body washed and immediately disposed of. The Christians wanted an open coffin display. They won. Art lay on display in a Harlem funeral parlor, powdered and preserved, a small cap on his head, as though posed for a vacation photo, or for the happy facade his counterfeit stage smile presented to his audiences.

While Art was alive, Susan claimed to have discovered—a bit late, to be sure—that Art was not divorced from his first wife at the time of their marriage. He had at least four children from that marriage, all of whom were known to Susan, including a blind daughter. When the beautiful redwood house was finally completed, Susan sued for annulment, based upon Art's bigamous marriage to her. Her lawyer was a former Vermont judge, and through his intervention, Art was barred from the house. Art estimated that at least $350,000 of his money was invested in that house—an investment that was to have no return other than what he declared was his love for Susan. I suppose it was love, whatever that grand emotion is. In Art's relationship with Susan, it was a series of wrenching disappointments. He was to have several other marriages: one to a Japanese woman, with whom he had a son, Takashi, and one to a Canadian woman by whom he had two children who, when Art died in 1990, were still infants. He never complained about his mistakes and was fond of saying, "Hey, man, in life there's no appointment so there can't be disappointment." He was quoting me quoting *The Unquiet Grave*. I always wondered if Art believed he was moving up in social class in marrying Susan, but that would surely be wrong; indeed, he showed some contempt for famous titles.

There was one titled individual, however, of significance in Blakey's life. The Baroness de Koenigswater, a member of the Rothschild family, seemed to be a person of inexhaustible funds. She practically adopted black jazz musicians, provided them with money and often welcomed them to her various homes as live-in guests. For a while she adopted Art. He could have had anything he wanted from her—that is, anything money could buy. There was no need to ask; she gave voluntarily and generously. She knew Art needed a large car to transport his drums and sometimes his musicians. She promised to surprise him and she did, but in a way that must have dismayed her. She knew Art had no interest in her custom-made Bentley. She presented him with a Rolls-Royce. Art rejected the expensive gift with some anger, lashing out at her, saying, "God damn it, you know I wanted a Cadillac!" And he got one.

Charlie Parker died in her Fifth Avenue apartment. Thelonious Monk suffered his last and fatal illness while living in her New Jersey home. Some musicians referred to her as the Baroness of Death. Among the many rumors and gossip that nagged her reputation was that she kept many musicians supplied with narcotics. In my brief association and contacts with her, however, she seemed only to be a gracious European woman who loved jazz and those who played it. Apparently, her children were the same—unobtrusively egalitarian and natural. Her *New York Times* obituary made no mention of jazz world philanthropy. It seemed much more impressed with her title and genealogy than Art ever was.

Art devoured life and, ultimately, life devoured him. It was painful to see this formerly robust and apparently indestructible man wither away, riddled with cancer. To the last, he refused to allow death to disturb his own expectations of recovery. Speaking in the grammar of a busy future, he was planning a trip to China and had a contract for Japan. He asked me to step down from the bench and accompany him to China. "Take sabbatical, man, it'll be a gas." It was as though he could relive the wonderfully incredible days in the

1950s when I was his baggage smasher, contract manager, and man of all chores for Art and the Messengers in their tours of Europe, Africa, Asia, and America. I was reminded of one of those trips, when Art spoke his mind angrily, instead of minding his speech.

He had a contract at one point for a performance in Algiers. He refused to say Algiers and always said he was going to Africa. He was as excited as though thinking about the trip was a new narcotic. It was in fact his first foreign tour, although he helped spread the fiction that his drumming and its sometimes primitive fury was a product of an earlier time spent in an African village. We had several weeks in Europe first, with two weeks in Paris. For the tour, Art had European style suits tailor-made for each member of the group. They were immaculate and a far cry from the later dress-as-you-wish style of jazz musicians—except for the Modern Jazz Quartet, who were always in formal dress and seldom worked up a visible sweat. As our plane neared LeBourget, a stewardess spoke to Blakey and asked him to be the last to leave, as his fan club and the press were waiting to greet him. Art, who had been sleeping, said, "Yeah, yeah, that's cool." Then he added, "Bruce, stick with me, my French is not too cool." He knew no French, and I was not too confident of mine.

As we left the plane, the photographers and press people, organized by Blue Note, clamored for Art's attention. His recordings had made him a jazz hero in Europe. Microphones, tape recorders, and cameras were everywhere. His worshipers had come to give him the kind of welcome that he had never had in America. I was impressed. It was obvious that to them that jazz was an important art form or Art form. Americans did not really understand jazz, Art said.

"The motherfuckers even called Paul Whiteman the King of Jazz!." He pronounced the name as two separate words "White Man."

He glowed as a reporter placed a microphone before him and asked in English "What are your thoughts, Mr. Blakey, as you land in France for the first time?" The French reporter pronounced the name Blakey as Blacky. Art glowered and said, "Listen man, my name is Blakey. I didn't come to France to be called Blackie." I explained to Art that the French "a" comes out that way. "I don't give a shit—my name is Blakey." For the next hour, the reporters struggled with pronunciation, monitored by Art. It was the peak of his European popularity. Until he arrived in Japan, there would be nothing to compare with the adulation and almost frenzied competition for his music and his frank comments.

Angry disappointment would finally overtake Art when he married his Canadian wife. It was a marriage I reluctantly performed for him. As with Susan, he was wholly dominated by Anne. A former waitress and jazz groupie, she knew the reputed preference black musicians had for white women. Her whiteness and her sex were her chief assets, although she exhibited a dogged devotion to managing every aspect of Art's life—even deciding which visitors could see him backstage after a performance. Unremarkable in her entirely conventional looks, she did reveal an artistic talent for creating an advertising brochure for the Messengers. She used her personal assets to promote Art's image as *the* consummate doyen of improvisational jazz. Art became her job and he was her product with a value to be maximized. She was good business for him. After Jack Whittemore died, it was through her hard-nosed negotiations that Art began to be paid more than he ever had before.

To many of Art's old friends, she seemed abrasive, hostile, possessive. She was a new kind of female presence in Art's life. It was said that she knew Art was sick long before anyone else. There was no doubt that she did an excellent job as his business manager late in his life and appeared to be successful in keeping his contracts in order and in keeping his money in her name. This was long after I had ceased to be his lawyer, and had become a judge. He never stopped calling me, however. There was always some question, always some invitation, always some temptation he placed before me to leave the "square life" and travel with him. Anne reinforced her take-charge position in Art's life by having two children in rapid succession. She was clearly aware of his love for his children by wives after his first childhood marriage.

Largely through Anne's promotional efforts, in the 1970s and 1980s, the world of music had begun to appreciate Blakey's greatness as a performer. European and Japanese promoters had to pay at last twenty thousand dollars a week for his Messengers. He nevertheless smarted because he knew some white musicians were making more than black performers. Always the social worker, the big-hearted caretaker of the waifs of jazz, Art would augment his regular quintet by employing those who were stranded in a foreign country, expatriates who were down on their luck. Whenever we were in Paris, for example, in the 1950s and 1960s, it was my duty to see that Bud Powell received a handful of francs, or anything else he needed. After a concert at the Paris Olympia, Art would have an enormous meal at some all-night restaurant and pick up the check of everyone. At least, I would, with Art's money.

During tours, before the era of Anne, I always held the

money. I paid the musicians, deducting taxes withheld. The same CPA who handled my law firm's tax records gave me a schedule for withholding taxes and social security contributions. After eight weeks in Europe, I had a special briefcase in which I kept francs, yen, marks, lire, and pounds. Clearheaded and alert as a tour neared its end, Art liked to think of himself as a financier. He would read the *International Herald-Tribune* to see where the best rate of exchange could be had. Once, he was convinced it was Belgium. He ordered me to fly to Brussels and exchange various currencies. Early one morning, I did, returning to Orly by helicopter with dollars. He ignored the cost of those flights, settling for the belief that he'd had a better rate for the dollars he bought.

Automatically, when returning to New York as though guided by some internal clock, Art would ask for the briefcase that held the cash, including all of the withheld taxes, the social security payments, and whatever else I had. This invariably occurred as soon as our plane began to descend to Idlewild, later to be known as J. F. K. I had to surrender it. It was, after all, Art's, except for what belonged to the government. I knew that the IRS would never see it. I knew that Art knew, also. The instant gratification of heroin would take most of it. This led inevitably to tax problems. His musicians would file tax returns and seek justified refunds, only to be rebuffed. From the 1950s, to the end of his life, he remained indebted to the IRS.

In 1958, when we arrived in Paris, Donald Byrd's group had been abandoned there by a promoter. In those days, all promoters did not provide round-trip tickets or deposit one-half of the contract price in advance. It was only later that the American Federation of Musicians insisted upon such a protection for its members. Being stranded, however, was not the poverty-stricken circumstance the word suggests. Each musician had his French mistress and lived in relative comfort and sexual compatibility. Walter Davis, Jr., then the pianist with Byrd, was a fairly typical example. His mistress was a young student whose family had fled Europe as the Nazis advanced. They had gone to South America and become successful coffee growers and exporters. Walter, following the standard practice, promised her that they would marry as soon as he returned to America and settled his affairs. "Affairs" was the correct word, for he had many, including outstanding promises to marry at least four different women. A marvelous musician, Walter gave promise of a fruitful career and a handsome living. He was having such a wonderful time in Paris that he was reluctant to leave. In the jazz circles of the time, heroin and cocaine and hashish were all plentiful. Walter knew the happiness and convenience of all of those sinful comforts.

When his lady finally despaired of his delay in returning to America and his lame explanations, she bought a round-trip ticket for him. Walter took it to Air France and convinced agents there that his mistress had used his money and made a mistake. He was not leaving Paris. He wanted his money back. He got it and bought more of his narcotics of choice. Finally, his lady bought another ticket, drove Walter to the airport and shepherded him to his flight. Walter really wanted to stay in Paris. He did not want marriage. In the States, he became the regular pianist with the Jazz Messengers.

Davis gave his mistress a false address and promised to write often. He wrote to her once, saying that the Jazz Messengers would be in Sao Paulo on a certain date and traveling throughout Brazil in three months. He had by then joined the Messengers. He knew at the time that the Messengers would be touring Europe, not Brazil. Such elaborate charades were not unusual among many heroes of jazz. They were young men of great ego and heedless arrogance encouraged by the beauty, passion, and worship of their enthusiastic claques.

It was as though they expected their vigor and genius to defy time, the erosion of narcotics, and the sapping exhaustion of the demands of each night's performance. In all my years of being a male nanny, caretaker, adviser, and creditor to so many, I knew only three or four who seemed to treasure their magical gifts.

Benny Golson, once the musical director of the Messengers, molded the group's personnel into an improvisational unity that made them speak as one without losing the almost savage purity that distinguished individual genius and justified the extraordinary fame of the Messengers.

Benny was incredibly sane for a jazz musician, but his conservatory background imposed no staid disciplines upon his playing or his compositions. He was so gentlemanly and correct in his deportment and character that I was amazed that he could perform and sweat and achieve such primitive ardor in dictation to his saxophone. It was a touching scene to me when, one Christmas week in Paris, the Jazz Messengers were guests at a students' party in a cavelike basement in Saint-Germain-des-Pres. Benny's model and the musical hero he most admired and whose records he most enjoyed and whose style he imitated almost unconsciously, was Don Byas. Byas, during Golson's time, had always been an expatriate, living in Holland, playing all over Europe. It was 1958 and Benny's first trip to Europe. Don Byas was playing at the student ball. As Benny was introduced to Byas, I could see the light that glowed in his face as he shook hands with Byas. It was the humble peasant being knighted by a great sovereign. Benny reveled in that brief moment's attention from the master. The touch of hands became a loving brand by the master's baton. It was a glorious triumph for Golson. He had met the flesh and blood of the recordings that had so influenced and shaped his own career.

Strange and unusual for a jazz musician, in the world of hard bop Golson was economical, sober, and businesslike. He would have seemed more at home in the magisterial dignity of the Modern Jazz Quartet. When the Messengers played in Vienna or the Hague, Benny was at home, comfortable in the history of all the great music that had been played there before and that he was then helping to make—in a different style, to be sure, but special in its own incredible creativity. Benny and I became companions of a sort, so far as a lawyer and non–jazz musician could be a close friend of a gifted composer, arranger, and performer. Perhaps I was starstruck. I was, I supposed, marveling at the nighttime adventures and Ms. Adventures of the young musicians. I could never understand how so much athletic endurance could come from those who seemed to waste life so generously. I assumed that Benny's role was that of a gyroscope or balance wheel, once the group began to perform. He endowed playing with musicality and unison without sacrificing the special and gritty inventive sassiness of bebop.

When the old francs were still used, Benny and I walked to the Eiffel Tower and he was told that it would be ten francs to go up in the elevator. That was about ten cents. He said, "Let's walk up", as he looked at an assortment of coins in his hand. We did. I was then in my forties and Golson was in his twenties. There we were: Benny, who never did anything athletic, and the aging lawyer, who fancied himself in shape. The climb told me a lot about vanity and the extremes I would explore to be accepted by the young.

Most of the musicians were suspicious of lawyers. It was the lawyers after all, along with agents, promoters, the record companies, the night club owners, and the tour producers who seemed to make all the money. The careers of jazz musicians were always being burdened by business necessities and the domestic demands of wives, divorces, and child support. Legal language, they believe, was not straightforward; it cheated, it plotted profits for others and deprivation for the unwary. Few admitted that they accepted the submission they cursed because it afforded them the means to appease one consuming hunger for another. Many of the young performers became addicts and learned with the adroitness of a medical expert how to find a vein with the needle of a loaded syringe. It became commonplace for me to walk into a hotel room to rouse someone who was already up. He would be sitting in a chair with a length of rubber knotted around an arm as he introduced a needle to a vein. "Don't shake the floor," I would be cautioned. The voice would be quiet, almost breathless, the eyes intently focused, sad and hungry.

The too-often-repeated scene made me angry and impatient. I believed they were wasting their lives and whatever made those lives meaningful. Addiction was a mystery that was to baffle me forever. And after a fashion, I was in complicity with the forces that would kill some of them. In 1957, Lee Morgan and Bobby Timmons, at seventeen, were little more than high school dropouts. Art Blakey discovered them in Philadelphia. They were then weekend performers, allowed to sit in with people like Philly Joe Jones, playing at Pep's. They were musical whiz kids, still learning how to hold a cigarette and look sophisticated. Blakey had an infallible instinct for finding young and truly gifted players. Morgan, busily imitating his master Clifford Brown, brought to the trumpet a kind of gutbucket blues tinged with a flaming rage. Bobby Timmons, his eyes seeming hooded or half asleep, made his piano brood with original fire. Measured for their European suits, as they prepared to leave America for the first time, they were wide-eyed, appearing almost to be a bit frightened. Sometimes, they shook their heads in sad amazement as they saw their fellow performers shooting heroin or inhaling cocaine, or smoking marijuana. Blakey smiled. "I'll have you guys turned on in two weeks, including my square lawyer." Morgan and Timmons shook their heads in the negative and mustered wan smiles, more bemused than anything else.

That was then. Two weeks into a tour of Europe, Morgan and Timmons were experimenting. At every stage door of every theater where the Jazz Messengers performed, one or more black expatriates would appear offering what was described as more exotic "stuff," "something new," or "It'll blow your mind". The next year Morgan and Timmons were what the people in "the life" called strung out—they were addicts. Morgan returned from a tour of Japan with a Japanese bride and could be seen on the corner of 135th Street and Fifth Avenue, near where he then lived, trying to sell his albums to raise money for drugs. It was a pathetic sight as he cursed white promoters of jazz concerts and festivals. It was ironic also since black jazz was not really supported by black patrons. It was controlled and segregated by whites. It seemed that something of this seeped into Morgan's consciousness. He appeared in the 1960s to have managed his drug habit enough to perform and to record, either as a leader for Blue Note, or as a sideman under other leaders. But until his death he remained enslaved to drugs. Arrested in 1966 for possession of a controlled substance, he told the court that he had private counsel and gave my wife's name and address. At that time, she had been dead several months.

It was often difficult to know if Bobby Timmons was under the influence of some substance, suffering from narcolepsy, or simply acting the role of what he regarded as a hipster. He was thin, and he never looked healthy. Neither he nor Morgan ever reached the age of forty. Timmons died in St. Vincent's Hospital, bleeding internally, his vitals irreparably destroyed, unable to sustain life. St. Vincent's became the very symbol of a deathhouse. Dylan Thomas, wasted by alcohol and perhaps by cigarette pollution as well, died there. Art Blakey was to die there in 1990, a unique survivor, as though heroin and cocaine had combined to preserve him for seventy years, so that cancer would execute its coup-de-grace.

Lee Morgan, unchastened by his addiction's savage consequences, retained all the arrogance of the star he was. His Japanese wife long ago discarded, he began living on the lower East Side with a woman he called his common-law wife. One night, his hubris betrayed him into a public dispute with her at Slug's Far East, where he was then performing. He was abusive. She threatened to kill him. He goaded her, urging her, with rash bravado, to do so, telling her she knew where their gun was. She left Slug's, only to return a short time later. Morgan did not know it, but he was blowing his last notes. He was in midsolo on the bandstand when she fired point-blank. Blood trickled through Morgan's trumpet. With a surprised look on his face, he slumped to the floor. For that killing, somehow misnomered as manslaughter and not murder, the woman received a seven-and-one-half-year sentence, only two thirds of which was served.

I loved Lee Morgan's music. I was angry that his arrogance had deprived me of it. But I still had Blakey, Bags Jackson, Horace Silver, Sonny Rollins, Ray Draper, Babs Gonzales, Jackie McClean, Nina Simone, Gigi Gryce, Benny Golson, Reggie Workman, Max Roach, Stanley Turentine, Mary Lou Williams, Roy Haynes, Abbey Lincoln, Charlie Mingus, Teddy Wilson, Miles Davis, Booker Little, Ted Curzon, John Coltrane, Coleman Hawkins, and all of the others who had passed through my office, in the bitterness and furtive joy of their lives, some of which were so sadly brief and afflicted. Naming them now is like reviewing a catalog of ghosts. So many are dead.

Eubie Blake lived for a hundred years. Three weeks before he died in the Brooklyn brownstone he owned in the Bedford Stuyvesant area, where he lived during his last years, Willie Jones took me to visit him. Blake said he had followed my career on the bench and wanted to meet me. We sat in his kitchen and reminisced. He said he had always wanted to live for a hundred years. But, he said, he had never anticipated the arthritis, the internal dissension of his vitals, the doctors more interested in his autograph than his ailments.

He sat there, his small frame wrapped in a bathrobe, recalling his great triumphs with Noble Sissle, his Broadway shows and his television specials. He was then recovering from his most recent hospitalization "I don't think I'm going to make it this time." He was sad and wistful. "You know," he continued, "I believe the thing I regret most is that my neighbors, my people, don't even know who I am. White people demand my autograph all the time." In less than a month he was dead.

Miles Davis, genius that he was, carried arrogance to new heights—or depths. When I first met him, I was at the Los Angeles airport with Art Blakey, ready to board a flight to New York. Davis saw some police officers approaching. He moved casually closer to Blakey and said, "Here, Buhaina, hold this for me." Blakey stuffed a small package in his pocket. The police, who had obviously been watching all of us, searched Davis and then Blakey. Davis was freed. Blakey was arrested for being in possession of heroin. My opinion of Davis was not to change. He once asked me to introduce him to a young woman. I did. His first words to her were, "What say, bitch?"

Davis's personal lawyer was Harold Lovette. Harold was more an acolyte and lifestyle imitator than a legal advisor. At the time, Lovette and I worked together. Whenever Miles or Coltrane needed legal advice, he referred them to me. He handled most of their affairs, managing business matters and their corporate checking accounts, through which he paid rent to me. Davis seemed to treat his jazz contemporaries with indiscriminate and uniform contempt. To appease the then new popularity of rock, he began playing in groups that used electronic devices and amplifiers. He thought black jazzmen were too preoccupied with venerating jazz as America's only true classical music. He sneered as he said he knew where "the money's at." He alarmed the jazz purists with so-called "fusion" record albums such as "Bitch's Brew."

It was the kind of clamorous keening that loft denizens of SoHo listened to as they watched light shows on their television screens. And they paid. He was their darling and he filled up halls and theaters. Producers gladly paid him many thousands of dollars for performances where he turned his back to forgiving audiences and often stalked off the stage when not playing. He had turned his musical back on such masterpieces of style as his own record, *Sketches of Spain*. How sad.

At Birdland one night, Davis walked up to a table, where his lawyer sat with his then wife, Frances, along with Cicely Tyson. "Lovette," he said, in his raspy whisper. "Take Frances home. I'm going to fuck that blond bitch over there." He then walked away. Genius apart, Cicely Tyson must have had then, if not before, some insight into the Davis character. It was, therefore, all the more astonishing when she married Miles. Nobody said a word. Davis often spoke harshly to his lawyer, no matter where they were. I asked Lovette once why he took so many insults. At the time, I was so naive that I believed lawyers were important, at least important enough to deserve some dignity. He uttered a melancholy confessional. He said he was from a small town in Tennessee, and when he first moved to New York and began to hang around jazz musicians, he wanted to be just like them. He wanted to have white women, own foreign cars, dress a certain way, and do whatever they did, including drinking too much and now and then driving his Jaguar onto the sidewalks of Greenwich Village. He was starstruck. Harold did some wonderful things for the musicians he represented. When he got a forty thousand dollar advance from ABC Records in 1960 for John Coltrane, it was a jazz first in terms of an advance. For Miles

Davis, Lovette invested wisely in blue-chip corporate shares, acquiring an impressive stock portfolio. In imitation of some of his clients, he dressed in tailor-made suits. His tailor was often in his office, as was his barber. At the time, Miles owned a foreign car. Lovette, therefore had one also, just a bit less gaudy. He kept a supply of marijuana in a desk drawer and never arrived in his office before 11 A.M.

One of Harold Lovette's constant visitors was a young white woman from a small town in Virginia called South Hill. Mary-Lou, as she was named, wore her hair pulled down around her head and face. She seldom wore a dress, but rather a military jacket, complete with ribbons. Atop her head was a British bobby's helmet, and on her shoulder there was always a monkey.

Mary-Lou had a daughter, Jennifer, almost eight years old. One day, she came to see Lovette, saying she needed a lawyer. He referred her to me immediately. She reported that she had been arrested for child abuse when she spanked Jennifer in public. Released in her own recognizance, she had a party that night in her Greenwich Village apartment. It went on into the night. At one point, the noise woke Jennifer. She peeked into the living room and saw about ten people, all smoking marijuana and blowing smoke into a paper bag. Mary-Lou would then hold her monkey's head in the bag until it had inhaled the fumes. The monkey, once released, would try to reach its perch hung from the ceiling. Drunk on the smoke, it would miss and fall down.

Jennifer, apparently appalled by such cruel diversion and the amusement of the smokers, went back to her bedroom, dialed her grandmother in Virginia, and in tears, described what she had seen. Her grandparents assured her that they would come as soon as possible. They drove to New York and complained to the juvenile authorities about what Jennifer had seen and asked for custody of their grand-daughter. Mary-Lou asked that I defend her and resist her parents' custody action.

Mary-Lou's father, I was told, was a confirmed segrega-tionist and the superintendent of a school district in Virginia that had separate schools for whites and blacks. In 1959, that was not unusual in the South. It nevertheless made me angry, a result Mary-Lou obviously wanted to achieve. When the trial of the custody case began, Mary-Lou's father sat sternly at the table of counsel for the City. Her mother sat nearby, now and then removing her glasses to dry a tear. Jennifer sat apart, with a social worker. Mary-Lou sat with me at a respondent's table in a West 23rd Street branch of the Family Court.

Mary-Lou, apparently trying to convince me that she was no run-of-the-mill southerner, told me that when she was in high school she had two boyfriends, one white and one black. One day, she denied her white boyfriend a date, telling him she had to do something for her parents. The boy secret-ly followed her as she went into a cornfield. There she met her black boyfriend, Sonny Boy Brown, and they made love on the ground. It reminded me of one of those John Dryden translations of Juvenal: "Many a wench has on a rock been spread. And much love had without a feather bed." They were denounced by the white boyfriend. "What happened to Sonny Boy Brown?" I asked. Mary-Lou laughed softly, saying, "Oh, he was never seen again." I felt a chill at those words.

Mr. Macbeth, Mary-Lou's father, took the stand and recited the details as given to him by Jennifer. The judge, obviously offended by the testimony, shook his head from side to side. The police officer who had arrested Mary-Lou for public child abuse was a surprise witness. After his testimony, he was asked if Mary-Lou had said anything. He replied, "She called me a 'fat cocksucker.' Mary-Lou dropped her eyes and shifted uncomfortably. I wished she had had a different hairdo.

In cross-examining the officer, I pretended, from time to time, to consult with Mary-Lou. In plain view of her father, I would go over to Mary-Lou's chair, put one arm on her shoulder, place my face close to her ear and tell her to shake her head occasionally, as though I was asking a question. Other than that, I simply moved my lips as though conferring. I could see that my black proximity to his daughter greatly disturbed Mr. Macbeth's sense of segregationist propriety.

Finally, the judge recalled Mr. Macbeth to inquire whether the Macbeth home had sufficient amenities to accommodate their grandchild, and nearby school facilities. Macbeth said proudly that he was the school district's superintendent. This allowed me to raise some discomforting questions about racial separation. The judge appearing impatient to end the matter, interrupted a repetition to ask, "Is there anything else you wish to add, Mr. Macbeth?" Macbeth, looking directly at me, replied, "On top of everything else, she got herself a nigger lawyer." Even the judge blushed and lied, saying, "Sir, we don't use terms like that up here," adding, "Decision reserved." I asked if he did not wish to hear summations or have briefs submitted, "No, no, not necessary," he concluded.

Of course, the judge could not then give custody to Macbeth without, in effect, rewarding a segregationist and confirming the description of me as a "nigger lawyer."

Mary-Lou subsequently reformed. She was not born again, but she moved back to South Hill into a changing South, then in the throes of desegregation; a world that her father never dreamed of and one that changed his role, if not himself. She became a girl scout den mother and enrolled as the only white student at nearby St. Paul's College. I had forgotten Mary-Lou by 1969, when I was invited to Virginia's Mary Washington College by one of the English professors there, to read my poetry. She was in the audience and after the program, she begged me to come to St. Paul's, where, she said, they had had only ministers as speakers. Reluctantly, I agreed, after she called various organizations on campus to make hasty arrangements. Virginia, as the bumper stickers said, may have been for lovers, but during the drive to St. Paul's in Mary-Lou's station wagon, a wide-ranging assortment of racist adjectives were screamed at us by the truckers and other drivers.

My speech was a disaster. It was in the school gym and, somehow, Mary-Lou had managed to assemble a large crowd. I touched upon the hypocrisy of white Christians owning black slaves. I invoked Langston Hughes's derisive comment on *The Ways of White Folks* and his remark that no one should expect white people to be kind to us since they are so unkind to each other. As I was applauding blacks for establishing their own universities and urging that no matter how accepted integration might become, black universities should always be preserved, the college president came storming into the gym, walked up to me, took the microphone and said, "Mr. Wright is *persona non grata* on this campus." Two of the president's security guards escorted me, one holding each arm, to my room at the guesthouse. From there, Mary-Lou drove me to Richmond, where I waited all night for the first plane to New York. As Mary-Lou told me, the white Methodist Episcopal Church supported black St. Paul's. And the president wanted no suggestion that his administration approved of my remarks.

Lovette asked me about Mary-Lou's recollections of the fate of Sonny Boy Brown. I told him that if he ever visited her South Hill home, to stay away from the cornfields.

Those of us on the fringes of the jazz world's frenetic excitements were shocked when Miles Davis summarily fired Lovette. It was the beginning of a sad decline. At the height of his managerial career for jazz people, Harold had added the extra "T" and "E" to his name, transforming what he regarded as a mundane "Lovet" into a more exotic "Lovette." Fired by Davis, his next setback was the death of John Coltrane, then at the peak of his career as a saxophonist. Early drug abuse had done fatal damage to Coltrane's internal organs. By the time the abuse ceased, it was too late. His almost religious diet of fruits and vegetables could not rehabilitate his damaged flesh. After Coltrane died, Lovette became the ward of whatever woman would care for him. Now and then, I would see him in my courtroom after I became a judge. I answered his questions and gave whatever advice I could. Always thin, he looked more emaciated than ever. He fought one last matrimonial battle with his ex-wife, who, he said, sold their Queens home and refused to give him one-half of the proceeds, before she moved to Florida. The father of two beautiful daughters, he saw one of them severely addicted to hard drugs. Harold himself seemed satisfied with alcohol and marijuana.

He tried to treat women with the same callous contempt that Davis used, but he could never really quite bring off such disdain. He wanted so much, though, to have a love life that imitated the multiple affairs of his jazz clients. I asked him once how he juggled his extramarital relationships and his life with Frieda, then his wife. "I keep her in Queens," was his answer.

Though Harold Lovette died early, at age sixty, he lived considerably longer than most of the musicians he imitated. The musicians, without realizing it, concurred in the bitter wisdom of Ellen Glasgow, who believed that love should be a passing pleasure and not a prolonged desire. Their basic philosophy about such things could be summed up in various tossed off expressions: "Hey, man, in this business, who has time for love? It's a mating of two sewer systems—just hips that pass in the night." To them, then, love was a bedtime convenience. It was seldom a matter of a vested emotion, a moral discipline, a long-lasting and binding relationship. There were exceptions, of course. Jackie McLean's wife devoted decades of love and support to him, making it possible for him to have a wonderful dual career as a performer and teacher.

At least, these international troubadors carried no baggage of sexual morality. They were not concerned with hiding behind some sort of Freudian theory or symbolic storytelling. They seemed to care nothing for the literature of guilt, if they were aware of such philosophical speculations. I wondered about their casual attitudes and relationships. I was always in awe of intimate relationships, despite my own tawdry record of multiple marriages. At least Blakey and I married them. During one of our layovers in Paris, some of the Messengers went to see a motion picture based on Mark Twain's *Huckleberry Finn*. They thought the slave Jim, played by the boxer, Archie Moore, should have been the star, instead of Huck. They did not like Jim referring to Huck as "Honey."

Lee Morgan protested, "I know Archie's no faggot." I wondered what they thought of Jim's disappointment in his love for the widow who owned him, but who wanted to sell him so she could buy a white baby of her own. And there was Huck, who fled from attempted patricide after being told that his birth killed his mother. I mentioned to the Messengers the analysis of one critic who saw all kinds of sexual symbols in the relationship of Huck and Jim. Jim was seen as Huck's lover, Huck's manservant, and Huck's protective mammy. The critic was ridiculed and so was I for remembering what he said. They found it sufficient to conclude that "Archie was cool, man."

I suppose I wanted to know why they were so comfortable, going from one woman to another. It was an effort to find out something about myself. At that time, I had had two marriages and would eventually have five. I never succeeded in making meaningful discoveries about the musicians or myself.

PART II

BLAKEY CONTINUED, AND OTHER MATTERS

Along the way, I became known as "Art Blakey's lawyer," mostly because he referred to me as that. Many musicians began to frequent my office, seeking advice. Few wished to pay. Some thought it enough to give me copies of their latest albums. Kenny Dorham, gave my oldest son, Geoff, a brand-new trumpet and flugelhorn, when I told him that Geoff wanted to take trumpet lessons. Apart from his use of drugs, Kenny was a consummate family man. He invited me once to his home on President Street in Brooklyn. At dinner, he dominated his wife and five daughters, all arranged around the table in quiet response to his orders. Horace Silver wanted to know if it was wise to move from his one-room basement to an apartment in the then newly built Park West Village, where Max Roach and Abbie Lincoln then lived, as well as Roger Ramirez. Horace was concerned about the increase in rent and the irregularity of playing dates. Sonny Rollins needed to discuss the future, any future. In 1963, he was just returning to the real world from a secret tryst with himself. It seemed that he had had a deeply felt religious experience. Our conversation went through a hot afternoon into the July evening. Suddenly, the lights went out and the air conditioning was off. "Shit," I exclaimed. We were in the midst of the 1963 blackout. The whole city was in darkness. Sonny remonstrated, "There, there; just a moment." I said, "It's a white conspiracy. They knew we were talking."

"No, no, no," Sonny said with some passion. "We are all brothers." He then opened his saxophone case and removed some white candles.

"They won't work for us," I said jokingly. "They're as white as the system that blacked us out." This seemed to anger Sonny. "My man, I told you we are all brothers." Our conversations continued by candlelight and would have gone on endlessly about God's existence and the joy of pure thinking. I pleaded other commitments. Sonny was *very* serious and otherworldly. Some years later, when I was recovering from a bad ulcer, his brother, a doctor in the Bronx, gave me a case of Mylanta to dilute the erosive acid of my internal tensions and disputes.

Booker Little, always quiet and intense, summoned me to his Mount Sinai Hospital room. He was in an oxygen tent. His white mistress sat beside him, her face stained with tears. He wanted a will. I took notes, prepared his fairly simple will and returned, found two witnesses and he executed it, leaving his entire estate to his father in Memphis. Booker had some small royalties due, mostly on foreign sales of his compositions. His mistress asserted herself so aggressively that his father abandoned the field to her and the will was never offered for probate.

For Ted Curzon, I had to deliver child support to his wife in Chicago. I met her in the airport and took the next plane back to New York. There was no Federal Express in those days. My fee: a record album. Ted was later to play a disastrous role in my life by being a kind of Dolly Levi in the Paris rendezvous he negotiated between me and the woman who became first my mistress and eventually, my wife.

Gigi Gryce and Benny Golson, who were serious about music and their careers in it, wanted to create their own publishing company. They formed Melotone and Totem Music. I prepared the papers and had one of the offices in my suite rewired to accommodate a rather large machine for reproducing music scores. Benny placed many of his compositions with the two companies, as did others. Melotone and Totem were to serve composers who were also with ASCAP and with BMI. At the time, it was thought to be a wonderful idea to insure royalty accountability. More than that, the black jazz composers would have their work placed with one of their own. After years of exploitation and disappearing accounting records, they had an opportunity to have two trusted and respected musicians as protectors in a greedy and predatory business. At least, that's the way it was supposed to work. It did not take long before rude commercial reality set in. Within months, most of the composers asked that their compositions be released to them. They made lame excuses, saying among other things that Melotone and Totem were inexperienced, even though they had come to them because of Benny and Gigi's experience and their knowledge of the business. Because of their sense of brotherhood in being victims, I was ordered to release whatever was requested. We began an investigation. For years, if jazz musicians wanted their music recorded by established labels, the record companies would often insist that some stranger's name be added as co-composer. In that way, royalties would have to be split with someone unknown to them, usually a relative of an executive. If there was resistance, there would be no record date. Black musicians were being told that if they placed their music with Melotone or Totem, they need not expect any record dates in New York. Eventually, the Gryce-Golson firms were left without music to promote. I lost a sub-tenant and two clients.

It was pretty much downhill for Gigi after that. Gigi changed his name to Bashir Quism and began teaching music in a Queens public school, so that he could have a firm base in New York and some income. He had placed his small son, then but a baby, in New York Hospital for what he was assured was simple and routine surgery. It was necessary to introduce a dye into the area of the proposed surgery so that photos could be made. A nurse allowed the dye to spill over onto the child's genitals and thighs, leaving substantial burns. Gigi retained a lawyer who, he was told, specialized in such cases, and began an angry crusade to bring to hell the doctors and nurses who had caused such a tragic accident. Gigi was never satisfied with the pace of the litigation. He never anticipated how the insurance companies could delay, demand, and examine. The wrong to his son seemed so patently wrong to him that he wanted instant justice. It was not to be. He retreated into himself and became a virtual recluse. It is almost as though he died of malignant hypertension and without resolution of his crusade to redress the wrong done to his son.

My happiest and most painful days were my travels with Art Blakey's Jazz Messengers. To hear them play was the joy; to see them devour themselves was the sadness. Some fled from America to Europe where they felt the air was purer, the adulation for black jazz truer. Blacks in classical music were perhaps more abused than jazz performers, since they were so few and so largely ignored. They were generally not allowed to practice their art. Leonard Bernstein, whose love for black youths was well known, limited his affections to the sexual level. He never used his extraordinary power and popularity to bring blacks into the New York Philharmonic during his long tenure. Black classical musicians were even poorer than those in jazz. The insult to them was constant penury and near-starvation. Everett Lee is perhaps the first and only black conductor to make it in the New York area. Even he was said to have succeeded, to the extent that he did, because he looked so white and, of course, had the mandatory white wife.

At the same time, black women were largely given free reign to exhibit their genius. Marian Anderson, staid, dignified, was almost a stern statue in the passion of her sound and movement. Late in her professional life, she was allowed to sing *Aida* at the Metropolitan Opera. Appreciation of the rare quality of her voice had to be separated from visual skin color. American apartheid was cannibalistic; it would and did devour careers and those who pursued them. She had neither the incredible beauty nor fire of a Kathleen Battle or a Wynona Mitchell for both of whom she pioneered. Serge Kousevitzky was stirred by the quality of Dorothy Maynor's vocal gifts. Critical reviews of Katerina Yarborough are scarce. She preferred the spelling "Jarboro." Billy Rose, the flamboyant impresario is said to have allowed her to sing *Aida* at New York's Old Hippodrome. While it was not the Metropolitan Opera, it was a first for black divas in America. Today, black women with gifted voices have realistic expectations about meaningful careers on the operatic stage, both in America and the rest of the world. Black males have had less success in that snobbish arena. *Othello*, for example, more often than not is acted and sung by a white in dark grease paint.

It was Dean Dixon with whom I was to have some personal involvement in 1954. At that time, I had only heard of him as a lonely crusader in the field of classical music. He was a latter day Chevalier Saint-George, the black invader of Europe's formal concert life who had changed his name to fit more comfortably the symmetry of the elegant circles in which he was, for a brief time, a dark favorite and oddity. Dixon would do nothing so superficial as to change his name. He was so desperate to celebrate the name Dean Dixon that before America's entry into World War II, he put aside his inherent conservatism to lead the American Youth Orchestra —which included an extraordinary number of blacks. America was then riding the crest of imagined American– Soviet amity in a unity of opposition to Hitler. To that extent, the orchestra was looked upon as a Communist by-product. It was a time when Dixon, despite his disregard for politics, was regarded as at least a parlor pink. Some critics of such camaraderie derisively repeated a critical jibe of the time; stolen from Coca Cola ads: "The Four Delicious Freedoms: The Cause that refreshes." Dixon's constant female companion was then Vivian Rifkind, a white concert pianist. Such interracial relationships were then regarded as sure signs of leftist allegiance. When he conducted, he always made certain that a piano concerto was on the program and that Miss Rifkind was the soloist.

Dixon's American celebrity was not long-lived. There was America's entry into World War II and its career dislocations. His name disappeared from the concert kiosks and most programs. The world of classical music resumed its virtual white-only comfort and exclusiveness. I came to know

Dixon by a rather indirect route. He was little more than a brave but peripheral curiosity when, in 1954, I learned that he was working in Europe and the conductor of Sweden's Göteburg Philharmonic. At the time, I had been goaded by Ramon Rivera, the director of the Harlem office of the Urban League, to join the board of the Protestant Federation. He assumed that I was a Protestant. He believed it was ridiculous that most of the Protestants in New York City were black, while the Federation's chief executives were all-white. My role was to shake up the old guard and give the Federation new life. I was an odd choice for any religious role, as I had long ago made it clear that I regarded religion as an emotional trap for the thoughtless. Apparently, it was believed that I was joking when I said I was an atheist. The quirks of changed attitudes were amusing. In the times of Christ, it took a brave man to be a Christian. Today, in an evangelical anti-intellectual society, it takes a brave man to have no religion or to ridicule Oral Roberts or Billy Graham. Those were the days when Rivera and I were trying to make the Urban League more of an activist body, so I joined the Federation with my subversive mission in mind.

One of the board members was a man named Spence, a senior partner in Spence, Hotchkiss, a Wall Street law firm that specialized in aviation law. We had spoken casually at various meetings. One day, he called and asked that I join him for lunch. He explained that his firm represented the New York interests of the Baron Mannheimer, a Swedish lawyer and philanthropist, who was chairman of the Göteborg Philharmonic. He said that there existed the potential for a harmful scandal involving the Baron's daughter, who was then pregnant by Dean Dixon. "Do you know Dixon, by the way?" he asked. I did not; not personally. Dixon was violently opposed to American whites, he said. I was not surprised. I knew Dixon's reputation. He was angry about what he believed America's white male society had done to him and his career. By then, he was married to white Vivian Rifkind, his former Youth Orchestra soloist. However, they had had irreconcilable differences and were separated. Spence seemed embarrassed as he touched upon sexual issues, but he continued. It seemed that Dixon, just before leaving America, had signed a separation agreement with his wife. It bound him to pay alimony and child support for the daughter born during the marriage. While the weekly sum was relatively little, Dixon never paid anything and insisted that Vivian knew it was never intended that he pay anything despite the fact that the formal agreement had been prepared by Vivian's lawyer, Maxwell Cohen. Cohen was well known to me as a lawyer for musical artists and record companies. Dixon now needed a quick divorce so that he and the Baron's daughter could marry before the daughter's child was born. To do so, Vivian's consent in writing was necessary. While Vivian was willing, she said the payment of all arrears was also necessary.

Dean was outraged. He wrote to Vivian that "their" child was not from his sperm and that she knew it. He accused her of having had many black lovers and that he had long believed that one of them was the father of the child. He was adamant and adversarial as the crisis deepened. Spence had been ready to fly to Sweden and talk to Dixon, but the Baron advised against that course, saying that Dixon would never speak to an American white. Spence and the Baron had agreed that a black lawyer might have some success with Dixon. Dixon protested that he did not have the money the agreement said was owed—over a hundred thousand dollars at the time. If that figure could be negotiated downward, the Baron was prepared to pay it, as well as for the divorce. Would I be willing to speak with Vivian's lawyer and then visit Dixon, all within a week? Spence said that as I was a partner in my small law firm, I would be paid a partner's hourly rate, plus all expenses and first class transportation. I agreed and asked that travel arrangements include a return by way of Paris.

The offer of a fee was generous by my standards. But it would not be easily earned. Vivian's lawyer, Maxwell Cohen, had obtained a default judgment against Dixon and was seeking its enforcement by having Dixon's conducting fees and recording royalties attached at every box office in European countries that recognized American judgments. It severely limited the places where Dixon could conduct or make recordings. Since our paths had crossed in other matters, Cohen and I could communicate easily. We spoke of the critical agreements necessary prior to my departure. He relayed our talks to Vivian. She seemed reasonable. She finally agreed to accept one hundred thousand dollars in cash, an enormous amount at that time or, for me, at any time. I was off to Sweden with what I believed was the good news. At least I had a negotiable figure.

Baron Mannheimer met me at the airport. While extolling the virtues of the man he regarded as his future son-in-law, he was troubled by Dixon's vehemence at the mention of Vivian's name. The matter was delicate, he said, but with some degree of diplomatic subtlety, I might make some progress. I was not a diplomat.

Dixon wore a dour mask as we were introduced. He was

as European as a non-European black could get. He wore his hair full-length, long before the so-called Afro became popular. He would not have liked the term "Afro". He resembled the busts of a stern Beethoven in his hard and angry countenance. I let him have the news of Vivian's demand. The Baron seemed delighted. Dixon protested: "You must understand, of course, that the child is not mine," he began. Without realizing the phonetic ambiguities and pun possibilities of his language, he said "This is sheer blackmail; I'll have no part of it. It's simply another American plot." In the 1940s, he had insisted that any American orchestra he conducted *must* have some black musicians. After that, nothing had come his way. His politics, of which he had none, became suspect. I wondered what he thought of jazz, the art form that so many believe is a black monopoly. I was afraid to ask, for it was obvious that none of Huxley's "little black nigger corpuscles" jigged in his veins.

And now, the protégé of a prominent white male, cherished by whites in Europe, Dixon was in his element. At least the Baron was not American. In the United States, Dixon's ambition had isolated him. Very few, if any, blacks were conductors, or sought to be. But there were many black instrumentalists who were conservatory trained. Most of them eventually turned to jazz as a matter of survival. But Dixon persisted in following his classical star. He moved with apparent comfort in what was pretty much an all-white world. He spoke its language and read its music. If Kousevitzky was then the royal chieftain of American music, Dixon was that conductor's self-endowed separate-but-equal clone. But he was energized by a monomaniacal anger at a system that drove him from his homeland to seek honors and rewards in a foreign land that he felt were his normal entitlement in any land, including his own.

Dixon invited American prejudice when he married Vivian Rifkind. It was an act of defiance in which he delighted. It was a ceremony that neither family wanted. She was a concert pianist who was ranked somewhat higher as a young comer than Dixon was as a conductor. He was considered as something unusual, a curiosity, a brazen exception to long-honored roles for blacks, perhaps a genius, certainly arrogant. At least Vivian was Jewish, Harlem's gossip went, suggesting that they were both probably communists.

The Dixon–Rifkind marriage was doomed. Dixon was jealous and suspected Vivian of indiscriminate affairs with black lovers. Critical appraisals alone would have been enough to bring their careers into emotional collision. Blacks who noticed his career, believed he had forsaken them. Whites in the musical power structure ignored him. He had had a fragile American vision and found that it could have no artistic realization in America.

For some reason, I thought it was a good time for me to talk to him. He had been harried by box office attachments in almost every European country where he conducted. He had become in effect, a pauper in tails and white tie. He was the welfare ward of the Baron, a status that embarrassed his sense of independence and humiliated him. Vivian had had the alimony and child support arrears reduced to a debt that was increasing each week. Box office receipts and record royalties continued to be attached and seized. Ironically, Dixon was conducting for Vivian's profit. He could not hide. His concerts were widely publicized. He was an attractive curiosity, something he hated. In his prim and precise diction, as though English had become a second language, he said his color had no bearing on his musicianship, making it neither different nor better. Except in those few countries that had no reciprocal agreements with the US, Vivian's agents were relentless in their pursuit and their warrants. The gossipy world of music kept Vivian informed of Dixon's career. She had heard of Dixon's affair with "a Swedish woman"—not just a Swedish woman, but the daughter of a wealthy baron. It was then that she set a price on her agreement to a divorce. Before that, she had ignored his requests for freedom. Now she wanted that hundred thousand dollars.

Dixon seemed to believe that if he condemned Vivian enough, things would turn out as he wished. I argued with him, cajoling, persuading, insisting. It was all so unfair, he said. It was extortion from the Baron. Vivian already had more than she was entitled to just by taxing so many box office receipts that included his pay. Finally and surprisingly, he said he would agree. He signed the form of agreement prepared by Vivian's lawyer. She was to go to Mexico upon receipt of one hundred thousand dollars. The Baron had prepared a draft on his American bank. It was guaranteed by the Baron's Wall Street lawyers. I cabled the good news to my principals. Dixon seemed unburdened when I left. We were to have a celebratory dinner on my next visit to Sweden.

Not satisfied with his impending official divorce from Vivian, he managed to place everything in jeopardy again. He, too, knew the uses of cabled messages. At about the same time my cable of triumph reached New York, he was sending his own to Vivian. He renewed his expressions of doubt about the father of Vivian's child and congratulated her on managing to "extort" a hundred thousand dollars without danger of being indicted. That would have been acceptable, tolerable to Vivian, for she had become used to his bitterness about money. But, one line in his cable was beyond tolerance, beyond forgiveness. He added: "You join a select group of musicians, for you can now claim the rare distinction of having been an artistic failure on two continents." A bomb would have done less damage. Unaware of Dixon's artistic rashness, as I relaxed in Paris, I was unprepared for Spence's long face when I reported to his office expecting applause for a successful mission. I read a copy of Dixon's cable. Vivian was now demanding what she said was the full amount of the arrears. In hard negotiation with her lawyer, I insisted that our agreement should be honored, or his client might get nothing. In the end, it was Vivian's lawyer who relented. She yielded, but never forgave Dixon. And I never heard from Dixon again.

After the war in Europe, Alta Douglas, wife of Aaron Douglas, asked Langston Hughes to look at some of my poetry. Hughes did so and said encouraging things. He was the only person whose cigarette smoking I could tolerate. He was always surrounded by clouds of smoke as he worked. He made a living at poetry and his writing after he left the Merchant Marine. He used his influence to see that my poetry appeared in various collections and small short-lived quarterlies. He persuaded Howard Swanson to write me for permission to put some of my war poetry to music. Swanson was then composing his *Songs of Death*, he said. I was flattered. Death itself intruded when Swanson suddenly died. I had watched death keep its Samarran appointments with jazz people from time to time. When Bud Powell was dying and seemed so fragile and weak, he wanted to prove that Thomas

Wolfe was wrong: he wanted to go home again after his long residence in Europe. One night after a long Jazz Messengers concert, I was backstage packing Art Blakey's drums. Powell sat quietly in a corner, simply staring straight ahead. His little son wandered about curiously. It was 2 A.M. Suddenly, Bud called his child over, placed his mouth over the child's and began to inhale, as though seeking a transfusion of youth. It did not work. He and Buttercup, the mother of his child, returned to New York, where Bud died. Soon thereafter, Buttercup died. With her death there also died any chance the child had to prove who his father was.

My long interlude with people of music had been a riotous classroom: sometimes sad, sometimes joyous, as I got to know those who could do so well what I could never do. While Art Blakey was often cruel and mean, he did far more that revealed great nobility. He was negligent where his first set of children was concerned. They suffered in poverty during their early years. Yet it was Art, Jr. who followed his father as a drummer. His daughter Evelyn also opted for music and dance. And, until her last days, Gwen, his eldest, treasured the honors that came her father's way. In that first visit to Africa, he was wide-eyed, especially since he had never been out of America before 1966. He expressed excitement about going to Africa for the first time. He was thrilled at the prospect of performing in Algiers, although when we arrived, the signs were not good. Our hotel was under tight security. The French and Algerians were at war. Whenever we entered the hotel, we were searched. Art's Muslim name made him suspect in the eyes of the French, a curiosity to Moslems.

The Jazz Messengers reported to the theater for the evening's performance. I had set up Art's drums. It was fortunate that I was in shape. I was not young, and lifting drum cases was a taxing chore. The theater, including balconies, was full. The crowd cheered and yelled as Art took the microphone to introduce the members of what he called his "Aggravation." Suddenly, he stopped. He ordered the curtain pulled. "Bruce," he summoned, "get the producer. This is my first visit to Africa and I don't see no real Africans out there; everybody's white. What kind of shit is this?" I found the producer at the box office. Perceiving disaster, he hastened to Blakey, to be confronted by the question: "Where are the Africans?" In the meanwhile, the audience had heard why there was no music. It began stomping the floor and kept up a rhythmic hand clapping. The producer told Art that black Africans could not afford tickets to the concert. "Bruce," Art said quietly, "give the man some money so he can go and bring some real Africans here—some real ones." And he added, "If you want a concert, you'd better get some real ones."

The producer, trembling and pale, took the money I gave him and disappeared. After about 30 minutes with the audience noise increasing, I peeped through the curtain and saw about ten black Africans herded into the theater. They sat down on the floor in front of the front row. I doubt that they could see the band. They could hear it. Art peered through the curtain and said, "Okay, let's hit it." The curtain went up and the music began. So did a storm of coins onto the stage, accompanied by catcalls and obscenities. Art stopped the music, took a microphone and spoke in English, the only language he knew. "Now, you people are supposed to be civilized. If you want to hear music, then listen. If you want to be savages, then we'll just pack up and leave. I don't need your money. I get more for one concert than your mayor makes all year."

I was unaware of the course of Art's financial data. The place became silent. The Jazz Messengers played for two uninterrupted hours. Art announced each number. There was no applause, just utter silence. At the end, the curtain fell and I began to take the drums down and put them in the cases. We left the theater only to be pelted with tomatoes, oranges, eggs, and even some stones. The Messengers ran for our bus. I could not run, carrying equipment. We were splattered. A bus window cracked, but did not break. No one said a word until we all got inside.

"Those motherfuckers are crazy," Art said.

It was a joyless African "homecoming."

We returned to Europe.

In Berlin, about to perform, and by chance off drugs for a few days, Art became ill with withdrawal pains. I was dispatched to find a druggist who might give me something to ease Art's agony.

In the meanwhile, the audience was restless and yelling over and over again, "Blakey, Blakey, Blakey."

Art, in obvious and acute discomfort, dragged himself to the microphone to address his audience. "All right," he said, "You want Blakey, well here he is. Art Blakey, Jr."

His son had been traveling with us. He played his father's drums for the rest of the concert. The audience felt deprived. Junior was not his father and never could muster enough of the original Blakey fire to take his father's place.

After 1960, I only travelled occasionally with jazz musicians. I devoted myself to my law practice. I left the jazz world, except to represent performers now and then and to share their pain. They seldom followed my advice. When Max Roach and Charlie Mingus wanted to sell all rights to a record made in Canada at Massey Hall, and called the greatest jazz recording every made* I sought in vain to persuade them not to. Mingus said if he ever wanted it back, he would check into Bellevue Hospital's mental ward and claim he was insane at the time. Both he and Max needed money, as they always did in those days. None of us could foresee that Mingus would die early and that Max would win a genius award of over three hundred thousand dollars from the MacArthur Foundation. At the time, Max and Abbey Lincoln were living at Park West Village, where all kinds of musicians and others were frequent visitors. The apartment celebrated their distant vision of Africa. Maya Angelou was also a visitor, along with many others. The musicians had a heartwarming fellowship, a brother-and sisterhood that knew their own artistic worth. Yet, living dangerously, they seemed terribly careless about their greatest assets, their talent.

In the spring of 1966, many black musicians were unhappy with the way in which the promoters of the Newport Jazz Festival selected its performers. They decided to stage a rump festival of their own in Manhattan. I was recruited to locate a suitable theater and arrange for its rental. The East 76th Street Theater was selected. It was small, but it was in Manhattan. It was to be a profit-sharing event. Coleman Hawkins, Abbey Lincoln, Art Blakey, Max Roach, Charlie Mingus, Papa Jo Jones, Walter Davis, Jr., and others joined the effort. We foresaw the making of powerful statement.

Despite advertisements and the top quality of the

* Charlie Parker, Dizzy Gillespie, Charles Mingus, Bud Powell, and Max Roach.

performers, there were never more than ten or twelve customers in the audience. The week was a total disaster. Max was so insulted he became a raging madman. He looked for solace in alcohol. He lost control. Abbey Lincoln's sister was visiting from California with a little baby. Max was seen placing the child on a bar in the neighborhood as though its formula should be 80-proof Scotch. The fiasco placed Max in a hospital. He was to emerge a different person. His genius intact, he composed the *Freedom Now Suite* as though writing music and lyrics for the Civil Rights movement then beginning to stir all of America. One brilliant trumpet solo, "On A Sunny Afternoon," could have become a popular success and moneymaker for Max, but he would allow no tampering with his inspiration. A man of extraordinary creative gifts, Max could make drums sing and waltz. He literally exacted melodies from his array of percussion objects. It is always a dizzying display to see each foot and each hand performing a different function resulting in an incredible coherence, a statement, a deeply felt meaning, an eloquent mystery.

Jazz musicians lived within a culture all their own. Relaxed when not on stage, they seemed like puppies, snarling and grimly playful, but with no hurtful intentions— yet still, tensely competitive. My office was often their brief stage as they met, making entrances and exits. One day, I introduced Joseph Warde, a new young lawyer, to Bags Jackson, who was then in the midst of his success with the Modern Jazz Quartet. Bags was the member who made it swing. Warde had always found something to say to each musician he met. He exclaimed proudly to Bags.

"Oh, Mr. Jackson, I saw you once when you were with a big band at Carnegie Hall. You played my favorite 'Bag's

Groove' in a new arrangement . . . I know all of your work," he rhapsodized. "I remember another concert at Carnegie Hall . . ." Warde would have run on at greater length and admiration, but Jackson, staring straight at him, said, "Wait a minute, man. I know all that. Goddamm it, I was there; you don't need to tell me that."

Warde was unfazed. He was thrilled to meet someone he had seen on the stage at Carnegie Hall. He could now claim he had had a face-to-face chat with Bags Jackson. He looked on in amazement one afternoon when Miles Davis entered the office while Max Roach and I were talking. Cheerfully, Max said, "Hey, baby, how're you doing?"

Davis looked at Max, a scowl on his face, as he rasped, "Motherfucker, do you think I'm going to tell you how I'm doing until you tell me how you're doing. Shit." Then Davis passed majestically on.

I missed seeing and hearing the voices of the music makers when I decided I had to move on. I needed clients who could pay and would pay. I had sons in an expensive private school preparing for an even more expensive college. I marveled at the survival of some musicians. Survival became a miracle. One musician, his eyes nearly closed as he teetered unsteadily, came to my office, he said, to meet Babs Gonzalez. I was then representing Babs in a civil lawsuit. Invited to have a seat, the musician asked if I would help him find a chair. He added, "I've been shooting heroin, snorting coke, smoking pot, drinking brandy, and waiting for them bells to ring."

It's ironic that so many wonderful musicians have lived such brief and dissonant lives. John Leonard captured a fitting metaphor for the way of life of so many when he wrote, in a wholly unrelated article, that something made as much sense as the Captain of *The Titanic* telling the passengers of that doomed vessel, "We're just stopping to take on ice."

In 1959, I met Fernando Howard, a remarkable and bright young lawyer. Formerly a robust and athletic man, he had been suddenly stricken with a mysterious malady that had crippled him in the way that polio had ruptured so many youthful lives. He walked—or rather, struggled—with a special cane. His spastic condition made every movement, even writing, an energy-sapping effort. His intellect was unaffected and, if anything, sharpened. He had the kind of mind I loved. Aware of the ambiguities of language, his wit was biting and leavened by humor. Sitting and drinking, he was a youthful guru, to whom I, his elder, looked for subtle and elusive insights. When I would complain that religion was an anti-intellectual affliction he would quote Horace Walpole's view that thinking could only make life seem ridiculous, while feeling made it tragic. He was a large man, always with fulsome ideas about everything.

Fernando came to my office looking for a job. He had heard that I represented a number of jazz musicians. He was a jazz aficionado. He wanted to discuss both certain and uncertain projects. He knew that many jazz performers had no business sense at all; except for occasional work and recording sessions, they led directionless lives. He felt they were exploited, used, cheated, and dictated to by record companies and exploiting entrepreneurs. He wanted to manage and promote the black musicians, give them investment opportunities and some business stability. I reminded him that black jazz people seemed captives of a relatively few whites who controlled who played where and when, as well as what kinds of narcotics and how much would be available to their geniuses. We both agreed that Alfred Lion and Francis Wolf were exceptions to the general rule of exploitation. They sincerely loved jazz and its black performers. Indeed, they had made many performers famous through their Blue Note label, enabling a generation of jazz artists to achieve fame in America, Europe, and Japan. It is ironic that two such human-itarians should bear surnames of ferocious animals.

I was wary of any venture that would attempt to breach the wall of white managerial monopoly. In the 1950s, I had joined Roy Campanella and Jerome Becker in a project to help guide the careers of professional basketball players. We had flown around the country, sometimes in frail three-seaters and in dangerous weather, visiting universities, speaking to athletes about completing their education and planning their careers. Our emphasis to them was that sports had become big business; that injury could imperil their careers as per-formers, and how necessary it was to provide for a future that could provide for them. Becker had come to me to induce Campanella to join the project. He had sought me out because Campanella was then one of my clients. We began flying ath-letes to New York and talking with them over leisurely week-end breakfasts at sleek East Side restaurants, places that Becker reserved just for such occasions.

Quasi-bankruptcy was the result, except for Becker, a very successful lawyer. Campanella had achieved great fame as a member of the Brooklyn Dodgers baseball team and even after the auto accident that confined him to a wheelchair, had not diminished his business activities. In the end, it seemed the athletes were curious to meet Campanella, one of the first blacks to break into major league baseball. All of them

enjoyed our largesse and advice, and then retained established white agents. Jerry Becker, suave, persuasive, handsome and dashing, invested enormous sums of his own
money in the venture. He was much more successful as a
judge and as a high-priced lawyer when he left the bench. I
mentioned this experience to Fernando, suggesting that black
jazz musicians were of the same cast of mind as the athletes
and that they seemed to prefer white management. But
Fernando said he had plans for benefits that no performer
could reject. "What do we have to lose?" he asked. "We venture nothing, we gain nothing."

He really *believed* he could save black jazz musicians
from white exploitation and themselves, even from their
widespread addiction to heroin, cocaine, and marijuana, not
to mention alcohol. His proposal was to arrange jazz concerts
in the countries where socialism, i.e., communism, was the
form of government. We would start by visiting the UN, talking with delegates and cultural exchange people. Innocently,
we believed we could make headway in that fashion, for the
socialist countries spoke as racial liberals and had never had
jazz artists perform in their countries. The complications gave
bureaucratic red tape a new dimension for us, as I was to
learn.

Unafraid of the unknown, in 1959 I left the firm in which
I was a partner, eventually having to sue to salvage something from my partnership investment, a sum I reinvested in
my new career with Fernando. We incorporated under the
name of Cultural Exchange Artists. Our engraved cards
proclaimed our standing: Park Avenue and 56th Street. Our
stationery listed our law practice as having three partners,
Fernando, my then wife Yvette, and myself; two associates,

Joseph Warde and Garvey Clarke; and a California counsel, Franklin H. Williams, who then headed the NAACP's Pacific Coast operations. The forays with the UN resulted in expensive lunches, long conversations, hopeful promises, and then instructions to firm up things by going to Washington to confer with ambassadors. Fernando had recovered what in those days was a large judgment—in excess of fifty thousand dollars for injuries he sustained while a passenger on a Fifth Avenue Coach Company bus. He spent it lavishly. Our office had a stunning oil painting that cost thousands. His taste was exquisite. For lunch, he preferred the chic and expensive Henri Quatre Restaurant, with its fine wines and good food. It was an East Side refuge for the wealthy. One entered by crossing a tiny bridge over a reflecting pool. A violinist wandered about, playing subdued classical melodies. Of course, Fernando took a taxi to get there and return. "Relax, Bruce," he was fond of saying, "it's tax deductible."

Each of us insured the life of the other for fifty thousand dollars. The premium on Fernando's policy was prohibitive, because of his condition, one that had never been specifically diagnosed and named. We only knew its effect. The visits began—to Washington and the embassies of the Soviet Union, Poland, Hungary, all countries where American travel was not encouraged and, in some cases, was prohibited. Fernando's wife had to travel with him to dress him and be otherwise helpful in tasks that were routine for anyone else.

Our plan was to talk with the embassy officials and then visit the countries themselves to enter into cultural exchange agreements. Greatly cheered by the results of United Nations conversations and those in Washington, Fernando won the toss to see which one of us would visit Europe and conclude agreements for jazz concerts. Of course, he had to be accompanied by his wife. They left for Moscow, with Fernando already planning to transfer substantial accounts to Citibank, the same bank at 57th Street and Park Avenue that had rejected us as clients because they knew we could not maintain a balance of fifteen thousand dollars, as the bank demanded.

Upon arriving in Moscow, Fernando and his wife registered at Moscow's most luxurious hotel. He then went to the office of the minister of culture, only to be told that the diplomats in New York and Washington could not control the minister's appointment calendar. "We do not even know that you are here," Fernando was told. He was then instructed to call me in New York, so that I could call the minister's office to say that Fernando was there. Surely, such a comic arrangement of serious business had to be a sign that Russia's Communism would collapse. I made the telephone call. Eventually, Fernando made another visit, but not until he was made to move to an Intourist hotel, a move from luxury that would shorten his stay in Moscow.

The Moscow visit was a disaster. The minister was uncertain. Were the American authorities aware of Fernando's trip? Did they know its purpose? Did Fernando have the approval of the American State Department? Eventually, Fernando despaired and left for Poland, where he met the same kinds of questions, uncertainty, and refusal to commit understandings to contracts. His experiences reinforced my detestation for politics, both domestic and foreign. Ultimately, Fernando and his wife moved on to Algiers, where he believed he had entered into a motion picture contract to market a script entitled, ironically, *The Red School House*.

When Fernando returned, he seemed pale, exhausted, and spiritless. Not even renewed dining at Henri Quatre restored him. Usually voluble, he was quiet and withdrawn, endlessly reviewing notes he had made during his travels. Nevertheless, he never abandoned his efforts to become an agent for jazz musicians, as he envisioned new efforts for our firm, Cultural Exchange Artists. Our international telephone calls exceeded our monthly rent. It was before the era of the fax machine and we had cable bills and credit card balances that, to me, were staggering. In the face of it all, Fernando remained calm. He would sit at his favorite desk, an elaborately carved door made of Philippine mahogany, going over notes and the names and addresses of jazz performers, or meeting with agents and performers. Mary-Lou Williams was a constant visitor. I was summoned to Fernando's meetings with her to listen to her fantastic tales of the voices she heard and the reports from the dead that she shared with us. This incredible musical genius and Catholic convert believed in angels, signs, symbols, omens.

Not long after Fernando returned from Russia and Africa, I realized that our plans to be first with jazz in the socialist countries were not going to be the productive success we had tried so hard and expensively to make it. I would have to rebuild my legal practice. My wife Yvette had become a member of the bar and was practicing with us. She loved going to court, and jazz musicians kept her busy on the criminal side, as she struggled with the system to recognize that addiction was a sickness that had no proper relationship to imprisonment. Neither she nor Fernando would live beyond the early days of 1966.

Eager to sign up Nina Simone, a deft pianist and

ferocious singer who emerged as a threat of vengeance for every wrong thrust upon blacks, Fernando left the office early one evening, saying he was going to see Ms. Simone in concert and to speak to her backstage. He did that, left the concert hall, raised his cane for a taxi and toppled over. Two days later, he was dead. His parents, faithfully clinging to their evangelical and charismatic beliefs, had a brief memorial for him in a funeral parlor with an open coffin. Called upon to utter a eulogy, I was stricken dumb. Looking at Fernando, lying there in blind serenity, all I could do was envision his dreams, his plans and the cheerful grammar of the future and the hopeful adjectives he had used to describe our projects. It was too much. I could not say a word. Frank Hercules, married to Fernando's sister, perceptive and sensitive to my helplessness, rose and escorted me to a seat. The rituals went on and on, as though to appease the primitive emotions of religious waste.

MY YVETTE

Shortly thereafter, I had to call a doctor for Yvette. We believed she had a bad cold. I told the doctor she was allergic to penicillin and I left for my office. Within moments after my arrival, Yvette called to say that the doctor had injected her with penicillin and she was in painful distress. I must come immediately. I did. It was horrible to see and hear her suffering. We did not have health insurance coverage, but our family doctor said he would arrange for Yvette's admission to Beth Israel Hospital. We were simply to ask for him when we arrived. I hired a car and carried Yvette to the back seat where she could lie down. At the hospital, I lifted her slim body in my arms, went to the admissions clerk and asked for Dr. Clark Smith.

"He's not here," I was told. I reported the allergic and painful reaction Yvette was having to the penicillin, pain that was obvious from her groans and contorted features. The clerk then demanded $375 in advance since I had no hospitalization. Anticipating such a demand, I produced three hundred dollars in cash and wrote a check for seventy-five dollars. The clerk refused to accept the check, saying "orders are orders." Unable to summon words cruel enough to describe my feelings of hatred for the clerk, all I could say was, "You're just another Nazi obeying orders in the name of your crime." I then left, helped Yvette into the car and tried to organize my thoughts. Finally, I decided to take her to a hospital where I knew that a former college classmate of mine was a surgeon. But, even there, with his emergency help, Yvette was not admitted to a room for almost four hours. I simply sat, brimming with fury against everything, but remembering two lines from an e. e. cummings poem that memorialized lost love, speaking of "great writhing words as uttering overmuch, / stand helplessly before the spirit at bay." Later, I was told that the doctors did not believe Yvette would ever leave the hospital alive. I shivered and recalled the last two lines of the untitled cummings poem: "Then shall I turn my face, and hear one bird / sing terribly afar in the lost lands."

Yvette remained in the hospital, under treatment. Science triumphed, of course, but not for life. Finally, I was called by the hospital and told that there was nothing more the doctors could do for Yvette and that I could come to take her home. At the hospital, Yvette was animated and full of smiles. She seemed to believe that because she was going home, everything would be all right. I was packing her things, including a sizeable collection of books and other gifts from her friends and clients. Suddenly, she called in a stricken voice, "Bruce, Bruce, it's getting dark in here." It was a brilliant and sunny morning in March. I went to the bed and placed an arm beneath her shoulders. But she had spoken her last words. She had fought off death for four months, a new longevity record for one with malignant hypertension and devastatingly high blood pressure. She remains a daily presence in my life.

Long after her death, jazz musicians were in court saying that Yvette was their lawyer. Long after her death, I wrote this poem:

ENDINGS

That I have loved that woman
captured now behind the shrouds of canvas curtain,
scalpels out at memory of other beds.
The doctor, a prophylactic snowman, an icy statue,
gestures to condemn me away;
I am not of his calling
and now have no claim upon the body and
the blood now his.

My eyes trouble as I hear his movements,
his scientific trespass
touching where I have slept and tasted.
Drinking tears, I fumble at a book;
the words stutter;
the title reverses time and place;
I think of her request for Simone de Beauvoir
as she recalled her own memoirs of a dutiful daughter;
she had smiled at her recollection of her kneeling
days of devoting at the Church of
   St. Martin de Porres,
her days of obligation.
"I paid duty and imported nothing,"
she would joke, recalling her confirmation
and how sometimes she remarked how her
   Hail Marys
could never make her an acolyte
or custodian of the candle fire.
It was later that she realized and dared doubt
to mention how The Word becomes snared
   upon its limits;
she toyed with the heresy of God as woman
and invented new definitions for morals
and, of course, sin.
She had one jokingly thought of Paris as a temptation
from the strictures of the natural law;
the City of Light had become her unseen
   mirror of amazement,

and the tales of the war years that I told
worried at her Roman fundamentals.
The doctor, advised by microscopic clues,
was a stern Oracle refusing questions;
he did, however, bid me to be cheerful, prescribing
avoidance of the predicates and treasoned
  craft of doom.
A nurse admonished me to wear the false face
of each confidence and cheer
and so, risking fragile humor,
I pat her pillow, adjust the bed and ask
if the probers respect her royal blood
that once owned a Congo claim
upon the darkness in her veins.
It was a question of ashes I sought to swallow.
A Dracula of healing hovered
ready to plunge a greedy needle into an arm
that had always astonished by its grace of slim muscle.
Slaking at the crimson passion of her life,
the deed was done. Lady Macbeth, R. M.,
smiled and moved on with her warm loot.
I could feed her, an aide whispered.
It was a plate of bland,
an offering of unleavened flavor.
But hungers were elsewhere.
Other beds,
other ways.
In rooms of ebbing life, one's nose

is bludgeoned by the sanitary reek of illness,
and those who are well
are embarrassed by their health,
and they curse internally,
fend at guilt and pretend there
is no anxiety to leave, or how.
She smiles in her shrunken jeopardy,
taunting thoughts
that once bound our joy to the same bed.
love sometimes bangs upon an empty door
as we see life in all its dazzling colors
become discarded wrappings from a lost gift.

II

I marvel at the bedside seers
costumed in their starched immunity,
with their stethoscopes and Latin mixtures;
they presume to know our secret statistics,
the source of our red fluid,
how much to siphon from where and when
and how one pain refers its torture to another.
She sees my discomfort and summons a smile.
She could not see the deadly notes the interns made,
or hear their consultations, their lectures
and their focus on the faint graph of her survival.
The doctors measured their doses,
as false as Hallow'een devices;
the pills shown in their colorwheel array,

placebos pumped into her pause along the
    road to Samarra.
She sleeps. I sit. She stirs. I waver.
I stare, a watchman for disaster, ready to cry out
and help her summon salvation
from her Vatican totems.
I speak softly of the ribboned flowers
sent by clients whose concerns nag her to be well;
awake, she moves her lips
as though confiding to her Rosary;
she becomes a Muse of speculation about
    Caribbean weathers
and she speaks of the long rest she will take.
Impossibilities are always worthy of their mention,
like remembering what never was, or counting
promises that are the need of self-deception,
intentions that end their lives before our own.
We always envision the past as worthy of resurrection
and forget its grimace of harsh regret;
memory sometimes splashes beyond our depths
and gives us the fraud to renovate dead vows
until they sink three times at once.

III

"The parquet floor deserves a quiet pattern. Speak
to your Armenian friend." She has suddenly
thought of her living room, lying there in that
    clinic for the dying.

As though in a domestic conference,
we spoke of the pewter on our mantel piece
and how the landlord must be called
about the misconduct of the chimney smoke;
she spoke of the books at random on the floor
spilling their subjects all about.
"They should be catalogued," she smiled.
It reminded me of P. G. Wodehouse, his library
plots and country homes we would never have.
One friend had sent his own arrangement of
her favorite flowers.
An artist whose work was unknown to
    famous museums,
nevertheless had pompous theories;
he deplored the mix of paintings hung among some of
    her own glass-framed sketches;
such cultural miscegenation, he said,
was aesthetic sin.
He had spoken with the air of a guru of all easels
and he proclaimed that her pencil work
destroyed the urgent splash and mission
of what a painter's brushstrokes
were meant to mean.
Pretending to adopt what she called his cocktail wisdom,
she promised, with mock piety,
to become a more careful curator
of iconographic obedience.

She was impatient to go home and
*   rearrange the future.*
Showing a sudden athletic animation
that made an instant fraud of all the doctors,
it was as though there were no fatal mentions.
I could see she still loved energy
and believed that both she and I believed
that survival would obey the dictates of her will.
And so, we spoke in conjugations of another time
as though death can be tamed by grammar
or simply parsing the brutal syllables of science,
or just voicing visions.
Trapped between the image and the real, I chatted as
*   though a cloned*
*   ventriloquist and diminished something of*
*   my self-esteem.*

IV

She longed to go home to the brilliant palette
of her own sheets. And she asked about her
fireplace; it was guarded by sturdy andirons
and a blackened stoking piece.
She recalled a garage sale where she bought
a brass or copper vessel chased with runic symmetries
and thought to be antique. It was used for umbrellas.
And she asked after her jar of penny-wealth.
A curious concave mirror amused her the way it
*   gave back colors worthy*
of Alighieri's flames

and the lights of passing autos in the street
always seem caught for a second—
imprisoned meteors, before they fled
into the swift instant of their flight into the dark.
I listened to her concise arrangement of time gone,
her spoken pluperfect diary.
I felt as though I walked through a labyrinth
of secret chambers in an undiscovered pyramid,
touching treasures of both then and now.
The screen before her fireplace showed a filigree
of arabesques, or perhaps scarabs and unicorns,
all caught in some stationary purpose.
I had left her favorite coffee table book open
to await her endless wonder.
It showed the baffling shapes of
a Belgian's imaginings;
it was always near the chair she used for thinking.
The double-page revealed a strange Empire of Light,
a puckish ironic of Magritte
whose dark and menacing forms
   always seemed to loiter
to devour both shadow and the
   suggestion of valence.
He always made miracles of water
seen through easel windows, and his stone planets
could be seen hung in space, distilling shimmer.
He bathed the world in other times
as though it were the dew of Eden.

V

She often asked that I read to her
from some Fourth Avenue treasure she had found;
fear of tigers in the night was her pretty pretense
when we read Blake together.
The broken glass of such recollections scars me
as I wander through their buttresses and walls
and try to move my tongue and voice
to sing in dry lyrics to stars
that burn in their heedless time to light our own.
It was difficult to dwell on such things,
but I did remember how she loved Blake best;
she insisted that only a good Catholic
could invent such excellence of proportion and vision
and Blake must have been a disciple of Turner;
for they both had discovered the face of God
and purified the Shangri-La of heaven's guess.
She searched for ecologies of peace
as she parsed both Blake and Turner;
she believed they must have known the
secret astonishments of Stonehenge
through their own private mysteries.
She said Blake, Turner and Magritte
were so different from those Hispanic majas
who stared from Prado walls.
Hirsute artists, she said, had stuffed their canvases
with stiff poses and haughty stares,

conquistador dandies in forced postures
of breastplate bragging;
even their nudes were overdressed in Spanish paint.
She found offensive to her catechism
the naked bodies of Iberia,
prone dark ladies
stripped to expose suggestions of pubic sin.
The unclad myth of Genesis, she said, was different.
Such recollections whisper vain distractions;
I sits beside her bed, becoming her sullen moon
gazing down upon the doomed lover of my love.
She lies there, the warm sculpture of my doting eye
as I wish away the menace of a thousand
   thousand years
of broken jeopardy that gives each life
its stricken time.
She sleeps, or so it seems,
exhausted by her joy of speech,
unconscious of my pain.
Soon, a priest will come
to offer helpless comforts
of The Word in the rituals of a dead tongue,
reciting rote, a sacred mummer with
seminary advices of absolution and shriven flesh,
with miraculous medals to placate
the fallacies of pious illusion
and to sanctify the fire of flesh and the blood's heat.

He will make signs
and ready the room for the Silent Speaker;
that unknown presence who inflicts The Word
that slays rebellious life, that aborts
the instinct to resist
final meanings and strangled sounds.
The Word says rejoice
and The Word betrays the meaning of intent
and refuses to revive the happy treasons of life.
"How dark it grows," she whispers.
"I thought the sun was shining."
She believes she believes.
She smiles,
and the love that was Vesuvius in her veins
leaves a last lifted gesture
for my congress with a ghost.

— For Yvette: May 20, 1937;
March 12, 1966.
Estate Nazareth
Secret Harbour
St. Thomas, Virgin Islands
Summer, 1982.

JUDGING—AFTER SOME DIGRESSIONS

I came to the bench ill-prepared for what I regarded and regard as an intellectually and emotionally severe calling. Because I had never thought of myself as a judge, I did none of the things conventional political gossip suggests are musts for consideration. Those deciding on judgeships are, of course, the politicians, the district and county leaders of one party or another, sometimes described as the kingmakers. I was contemptuous of them. I mocked them in my speeches. I repeated sarcastically the fiction that over every club house door is the legend: "If he's talking sense, throw him out."

None of my beginnings, youth, or manhood up to age fifty ever suggested that I would become a judge in three different courts of New York City and State. It had never occurred to me to consider a career as a judge. In fact, I had always studiously avoided politics and public service, ridiculing both politics and politicians. I remain surprised that I ever became a judge. All of my earlier experiences have something to do with the kind of judge I did become, an assessment of which is better made by those other than myself.

Still, I felt proud when J. Raymond Jones became the first black Democratic county leader in Manhattan. In my youth, I knew that James S. Watson and Francis Rivers had had political and club involvement. They were impressive and dignified men. They owned their own homes and I envied them that. I had a baseless impression that they had no interest in poetry and literature; that any discussion with them would have to be about the legal matters they had handled and little more, other than how they had been lionized by the black bourgeoisie, a society I looked upon as an outsider and with awe and some envy as well. They were people who appeared now and then in *Ebony,* the black newspapers, and gossip columns, as smiling successes. They were symbols, and for some even role models.

Mollie Moon became another one of those comfortable symbols of black wealth, prestige, and integrated joy though she was no more than a lumpen civil servant. She had founded the Urban League Guild. She devised stunning masked balls in beaux arts splendor. She was always smiling. Her husband, Henry Lee Moon, ran public relations for the NAACP. I never understood how he could use the name "Lee," as I associated that name with the Confederate general of that name, America's most beloved traitor. General Lee had fought, so far as I was concerned, to preserve slavery. That one family, the Moons, it seemed, controlled the two most respected black organizations in New York. I regarded both with respectful homage. I felt honored that I lived in the same building with them in the late 1930s. I assumed that they were doing all of the other tenants a favor by living at 43 West 66th Street. This typical Manhattan walkup was surrounded on both sides by stables, and the smell of horse manure was unavoidable, especially in warm weather. And yet, it was "downtown," not a Harlem tenement—although a tenement, nevertheless.

Number 43 was owned by a black baptist group. The group also owned another building nearby on West 65th Street in which, by the way, no blacks were allowed to rent. But number 43 was the focus of attention, mainly because the Moons were there. The black press invariably showed her either arriving by air from some distant place, or just leaving.

Her travels were very impressive and I loved hearing her tell how she was met at various airports by doctors and others of equal distinction, and never had to face discrimination at some benighted hotel in the hinterlands. My friend Ed Morrow lived there, also. A studious-looking man, he had arrived in New York, surprisingly enough, by way of Deadwood, South Dakota. His family were the only blacks in that lonely town on the plains. I regarded him with the same wonder reserved for the Grand Canyon and the heroic sculpture of Gutzon Borglum. We had a private joke about how George Washington, the slaveowner, was lashed in stone to Abraham Lincoln, the emancipator. Morrow had another distinction as well, he was a Yale graduate long before minority students at great universities became fashionable.

While the resident intellectuals had the prestige, it was the superintendent, Mr. Brown and his wife, who seemed the most well-to-do. Mrs. Brown used their free apartment for her evening séances. She told fortunes at a round table draped in a multicolored cloth. The Browns were the only residents with an air conditioner. In those days, one could park on the block and impressive cars discharged their elegant passengers to hear Mrs. Brown's candlelit runes translated into whispered assurances. I heard that she even had a crystal ball.

My greatest disappointment in the building was to discover that Mollie Moon, in her travels to other states and to Puerto Rico, was not an independent black bourgeoisie frequent-flyer at all. She was a welfare department caseworker. It was her job to escort poor people back to their places of origin so they would not remain in New York on welfare. On such trips, Mollie checked on her national network of women's clubs and Urban League Guilds. Trained as a pharmacist at

Meharry Medical School, she never filled a prescription.

Some years later, but long before the Civil Rights movement and the sit-ins at southern and other hotels, Mollie became a client of my firm in a suit against New York's Pierre Hotel. Each summer, the Urban League Guild sponsored a fundraising event. Often such things were arranged by Wall Street lawyers, brokers, or bankers, whose wives were on the impressive board Mollie had assembled for the Guild. She decided that the Guild was so famous and well-thought of that she needed no white help in arranging the Guild's annual fundraising banquet. In a show of misplaced independence, she called the Pierre's banquet manager and selected a mutually-agreed-upon summer date for the use of the roof garden. When Mollie appeared at the hotel to sign the contract, the banquet manager saw that she was black and immediately denied he had ever spoken to her, adding that, in any event, the roof garden was being painted on the date in question. The banquet manager, a small pompous European, with the accent and exaggerated gestures and expressions that were often seen in satires and comedies of manners, was obviously a seasoned liar. Unaccustomed to such rejection Mollie began her own investigation of the Hotel Pierre. She did not believe that the hotel would paint its roof garden in the summer, the months of its greatest use. She called the wife of a Wall Street lawyer, one of her white board members at the Guild. Told the story of Mollie's misadventures, the woman called the Pierre ostensibly to arrange a private party at the Roof Garden. She was given the same date that Mollie had been told was unavailable. She then went to sign the contract, with Mollie hovering outside, in the background. As she prepared to leave to exhibit the signed contract to a smiling and triumphant Mollie, the banquet manager saw her. He addressed Mollie's white friend, demanding to know if there would be colored people at the affair. "There will be all kinds of people there," he was told. Mollie and her friend rushed out. The contract had been signed, "Mrs. Robert Kinkaid," with her husband's Wall Street address. While Mollie and Mrs. Kinkaid were out celebrating, the banquet manager called Mr. Kinkaid to cancel the contract, claiming that he had made an inadvertent error and that all subsequent dates were booked up years in advance. When she learned this, Mollie called my office, eager to sue. While she could not sue for breach of the Kinkaid contract, she had evidence of the racial discrimination against the Guild and herself. She would have preferred to be represented by the Kinkaid law firm; that firm, however, simply said, "We really don't handle matters of that sort," as though to be involved in such litigation would blemish the firm's white-shoe reputation.

By default, then, my small firm became counsel to the Guild. My then partner, Lisle Carter, was a brilliant lawyer of dark internal moods, who would have been a success without the impressive legal accomplishments of his mother. He won the Moon case, which brought instant attention and publicity to our obscure firm, then with four lawyers and one typewriter that I had looted in the former Czechoslovakia during my army service during World War II.

It was my uneventful practice in small cases and my prewar employment in an East 57th Street art gallery at fifteen dollars per week, that gave me any experience to be brought to the job of judging, a career that I had never considered possible. There was also, to be sure, my brief (a year or so) experience at the law firm of Proskauer, Rose, Goetz &

Mendelsohn, a firm then over one hundred years old. I regarded Joseph M. Proskauer with awe, as I did any judge, for the business of judging represented the pinnacle of a career in the law. But the things I learned at that firm, with my uncomfortable beginning as its first black lawyer, were not the everyday grist of my private practice later on. My friends at the Proskauer firm, after I left, did regard me as something of a *wunderkind* for having what they called the chutzpah to brave the unknowns of private practice. In those unenlightened days, one could labor in total professional obscurity. The law profession, unwilling to taint its presumed nobility with hucksterism, was not permitted to advertise. Becoming known was pretty much a matter of word-of-mouth from satisfied clients. But first, one somehow had to get the clients.

Former associates sometimes referred their maids or other employees to me. One such associate, firmly on a partnership track, made the mistake of impregnating his secretary. What could provide a more secretive and suppressed way of handling her claims than having the problem handled by a black lawyer, who kept matters at a discussion stage, instead of engaging in public litigation? It was all resolved, with considerable financial payments to the woman in question until the child reached the age of twenty-one. The associate became a partner in due course, after which he demanded that I surrender to him the entire file so that it could be shredded. By that time, he no longer trusted me, I suppose. The mother would, from time to time, send me photographs of the child, a beautiful girl. However, my secret client refused to look at her unless he did so inadvertently when I turned over my file to him.

The same lawyer, Jewish, tall, and handsome, appeared

to love Christian women. We remained friends long after I left the Proskauer firm. The friendship ended, however, when he set up housekeeping with a Protestant from Montana. My wife and I were invited to dinner at their apartment, as were two of his partners and their wives. During dinner the subject of the invasion of Grenada came up. One partner described how overjoyed his son was to come back to the United States. The son, he said, kissed the ground. That seemed so silly to me that I said how I always regretted returning to America from beyond the seas, in view of the racial climate here. My friend's lady, with eyes blazing, said in a loud and angry voice, "Bruce, if you don't like the United States, leave, just leave!" My reaction was that in that case, I would first have to leave that apartment and, I added, perhaps foolishly, "And before dessert, too! What hospitality!" That was the incurable breach. My friend became my instantaneous ex-friend. Obviously, he assumed that his lady had been insulted and he supported her wholly.

But I digress, except that I have always been outspoken on matters of race in the United States and elsewhere. My friend, despite his professional brilliance, success, and wealth, never spoke angrily about matters of race. He told me of a Christmas trip he and his lady had made to her family in Montana. In little above a whisper, he told me of sitting at the dinner table listening to his lady's parents spewing racist nonsense about Jews. He said that he never uttered one protest, for which I chastized him. "I don't see the point in arguing," he said.

After a friendship of more than four decades, I realized that he was an archconservative, reluctant to rock any sociological boat. It made my wonder how he had been my friend for so many years, despite my various comments on America the beautiful, and on racism of all kinds. I had had white friends with whom I shared confidences while I was with the Proskauer firm. Most of them, however, no matter how conservative their views, always expressed forthright opposition to racism. Even Jacob Lohengrin [not his real name], who seemed such an egalitarian, spoke frankly to me deploring the fact that one of the firm's corporate clients he represented would not hire a black driver in its business. Liberal though he was, he said he would try to get a position for a young black applicant at "a place uptown on 125th Street."

All of these experiences and many others formed the background that I brought to the bench, when unexpectedly, I was named to the Criminal Court of New York City by then Mayor John V. Lindsay.

This is how it happened.

In 1969, I was counsel to one of Lindsay's so-called superagencies, The Human Resources Administration. I had had that job for two years when I received a call from City Hall telling me that I must get over there immediately to see the mayor. I assumed that he wished to discuss the then ongoing investigation of Human Resources. But when I arrived, the mayor was with Percy Sutton, a former client, who had been borough president of the Borough of Manhattan. Without any formality at all, the mayor said, simply, "Bruce, how would you like to be a judge?" I was dumbfounded. I thought for a moment that I had not heard correctly. I then replied, "I don't have any money to buy a judgeship." The mayor replied, "You don't need any money." I then protested that I had never handled a criminal case, although I had argued criminal appeals in both the state and federal courts.

Ultimately, as though I still could not believe what I had heard, I said I would talk it over with my two older sons, Geoff and Keith. I then left and went off to the West Indies for a vacation. When I returned, I found urgent messages in my letter-box and I accepted. Thus, in February 1970, I was sworn in, marking the quiet beginning of a raucous and controversial career as a judge.

Involved in one controversy after another, over my bail policy for defendants arraigned before me—accused of releasing upon a hapless and fearsome public ruthless and vicious thieves, burglars, and rapists, I was pilloried by the police union and the tabloid press. My life was threatened, as were the lives of my sons and my wife. The black police inducted me as an honorary member of their organization known as The Guardians. They also provided bodyguards for me whenever I had to debate the head of the Patrolman's Benevolent Association. Various churches and synagogues demanded that I appear before their congregations and explain what they called my "conduct." Speaking invitations came from as far away as California, Arizona, the state of Washington, and the Dakotas. For several years, I was earning more in speaking engagements than I was in my judicial salary.

Outside my courtroom where daily calendars are posted, with the name of the judge presiding, someone had scratched out my name and inserted "The Nigger Judge." The court administrators, despite knowing that I was doing nothing other than honoring the spirit and the letter of the Eighth Amendment to the United States Constitution, never offered an encouraging word. Instead, the administrative judges devised oppressive schemes to "contain" and control me. At one point, I was assigned to a tiny roach-and mouse-infested room bearing the elegant title of "Youth Part." For many months, I met with youthful offenders, reviewed their response to ninety days of minimal rehabilitative exposure, and stamped "dismissed" on the files of those who had had no further infractions for the last three months. E. Leo Milonas, then the deputy chief administrative judge, looked in my hovel of a courtroom one day, deplored the conditions, and ordered that I be regularly assigned. After one week, I was once again reassigned to a do-nothing position. I was barred from deciding motions or conducting trials. My chambers were seldom cleaned and neither soap nor toilet paper was provided to my toilet. Community organizations reading about these things came to my chambers heavily laden with soap, toilet paper, and other amenities. Although I shared chambers with Frederic Berman, also a Criminal Court judge, he was seen there perhaps once or twice over my ten year tenure as a Criminal Court judge.

The PBA demanded that I be defrocked or transferred to a place where I would have no criminal cases. Whenever there was a case before me to which a defendant had been charged with assaulting or shooting a police officer, the PBA would flood my courtroom with its members. On one occasion they became raucous, laughing, farting and stomping their feet as I walked to the bench from the robing room in the rear of the courtroom, chanting in rhythm to my steps, "Turn 'em Loose Bruce," over and over again. This was a kind of well-armed lobbying and attempted intimidation, seeking to frighten me into doing what they wished. It did not work, of course. Eventually a sympathetic clerk, Eugene Hanson, had to threaten to oust them all and/or arrest those creating a nuisance.

In Brooklyn, when I was assigned there, it was the same. Once, I told the district attorney that if cases were not ready within the statutory period, I would dismiss them. This was translated into quite another statement and the administrative judge in Brooklyn reported to David Ross, then the deputy chief administrative judge, that I had said that as long as I was on the bench, "no black or Puerto Rican would ever do time." False though it was, Ross never took the minimal trouble to order a copy of the court's stenographic minutes to see precisely what I had said. I had been sent to Brooklyn, originally, to preside over an experimental Part, but I was now summarily transferred to Manhattan where, as David Ross said, he could keep an eye on me. Eugene Gold was then the district attorney in Brooklyn. It was he who attributed to me the fictitious and ridiculous statement that I would send no blacks or Hispanics to jail, and communicated those words to Ross. When I confronted Ross, he denied knowing Eugene Gold at all, and yet described him as a "piss ant," whatever that is, unless Ross, not known as an intellectual, meant "pismire," but preferred the more vulgar term of "piss." Anyway, Gold, as it developed, was revealed as a sex molester of the young and he was given a rap on his wrist and banished to Israel where, presumably, he is living happily, and perhaps, even rehabilitated.

Transferred back to Manhattan from Brooklyn, things did not prosper. The administrative authorities apparently believed I was a Christian, so I was assigned to Night Court in Christmas and Easter weeks, among others. I was hailed before the Appellate Division Disciplinary Committee and harassed about my bail policies. On one occasion, as I entered the room of the all-male disciplinary group, their heads were barely visible above stacks of papers in front of each one. As I learned, almost immediately, they were copies of my speeches. Since I had never made copies myself, it was abundantly clear that all of my speeches were monitored and taped and delivered to the administrative judges.

On another occasion, before the Commission on Judicial Conduct was created by the State Legislature, I was called before the Appellate Division's disciplinary committee again, this time for saying, in a speech at Princeton University, that white police officers seemed to believe that they had a license to shoot and kill blacks with impunity. That speech was described as "inflammatory," but to me, at least, it seemed true—since no white officer had ever been convicted of killing a black. It was thought that the drought would end when Thomas Shea, a white officer was tried for killing a ten-year-old black boy named Clifford Glover. Shea said he thought the Glover child was an adult robbery suspect. While saying nothing about simply killing a mere "suspect," Shea was asked during his trial if he could not tell the difference between a little boy and a fully grown adult, especially at a distance of just three feet. Under oath, Shea answered that all he saw was the color of Glover's skin.

In general, I was cautioned to be careful or, in the idiom of the streets, to watch my mouth.

One night in the Bronx Criminal Court, a young assistant district attorney, during a recess, virtually bragged to me about his sympathy for the John Birch Society, confessing that he, as a white person, knew that all whites carry with them the baggage of racism. Shortly thereafter, as court resumed, he demanded $25,000 bail for a sixteen-year-old black high school student with no criminal record, who had been arrested for stealing some phonograph records from Alexander's Department Store. Long after I had released the boy on his own recognizance, the young district attorney continued to argue for bail. Wearied by his repetitions, I suggested that he must be energized by some kind of racial bias, in view of his confessions to me during the recess. He rushed up to the bench and said, "I told you those things in confidence." Either he or one of his confederates then called *The Daily News* to report the incident. At one point during the district attorney's argument, I admonished him, saying that stealing record albums was not the worst crime in the world. The next day, *The Daily News* had a headline that said, "Judge Says Stealing Is No Crime." So much for objective reporting. Once again summoned before a disciplinary hearing, the committee members began questioning me about what I had said to the district attorney. Each member had before him a transcript of the exchange. I had none. They were compelled to grant a brief adjournment, so that I could read the transcript. In preparation for that hearing, I had sought to get a copy of the transcript. The court reporter told me that he had orders not to allow me to have a copy.

After one particularly nasty confrontation before the judiciary Relations Committee, Albert Richter, the Committee's prosecutor of charges against me, wrote an unsolicited letter to me. His wife was a young Legal Aid Lawyer who had appeared before me several times. Her favorable opinion of my conduct on the bench apparently inspired his rather remarkable letter, written in his own hand. I reproduce it in its entirety:

"Dear Judge Wright,

About two hours ago it came to me in a rather discon-certing flash, that I owe you an apology, long overdue, for my participation as counsel for the Judiciary Relations Committee in the "investigation" conducted against you several years ago. It would take too long to describe in this letter the mental processes that precipitated this realization on my part, but I can tell you it was two movies I recently saw: "The Year of Living Dangerously" and "Bananas" that set me to re-examine certain premises I had held about "law and order," racism, and the terrible forces sometimes unjustly unleashed by the government and certain ugly segments of the press against individuals who rock the boat to upset the establishment.

I am happy—or perhaps more accurately profoundly relieved—that you persevered through it all, and that the public is still the beneficiary of your judicial services and conscience. Through it all you consistently maintained a pride and dignity that I shall always remember and admire. It was an understatement to acknowledge that the circum-stances and pressures were trying; and I have little doubt that most men would have buckled or retreated. There was an hysterical mob screaming for your blood because you had the temerity to remind us that racism still lives like a cancer in our society, and that when we treat poor blacks accused of crimes as "niggers" to be thrown into over-crowded cages like animals and not looked at again—then we are committing a crime against humanity. You had the audacity to demand that we open our eyes and see.

There was, as I recall, no great public outcry or investi-gation into three horrible conditions you so vividly described; instead the focus was on the "unjudicial" language you used when you described them.

I now realized that those were bad times for me, but surely they were far worse for you. I am sorry for the pain you had to bear in the course of that miserable episode, and for whatever part I played in it. I hope you will forgive me.

Sincerely,

Albert Richter

P.S. Some good had already arrived just from the idea of writing this letter. I asked a friend in the courthouse—who happens to be black—whether I should stir these old memories up. He said "You've got to, because you're a class act." That was one of the nicest things anyone ever said to me.

— A.R.

Then came the Mia Lancaster incident in my life, as a result of which the Committee on Judicial Conduct sought to defrock me and recommend that I be dismissed from the bench. During my career, I met a young lady named Mia Lancaster, then a model. I admired her ability to argue and present a case. She had been accused of an assault, or having arranged an assault against a former boyfriend. She also wanted to be reemployed as a model. She had been fired as a result of the criminal charges brought against her. I wrote at least two letters attesting my knowledge of her character and urging that she be reemployed.

Some years after that, when I was sitting as a justice of the State Supreme Court, Ms. Lancaster appeared before me again. She was then prosecuting a civil action against her former lover and she was moving for interim relief of some kind. Her opposition, who later said he was aware that I knew her, made his argument against her application. I decided the motion against Ms. Lancaster and forgot about the incident. I had also gone to her home, a one-room studio apartment on the East Side. Fortunately, for me, I had gone with my wife. We were supposed to have dinner and to meet Ms. Lancaster's then current boyfriend, the actor Yul Brynner.

I doubt that the Judiciary Relations Committee knew that I had been with my wife at the time. Under the direction of its attorney-in-chief, a former assistant district attorney, Gerald Stern, the Committee became known as "The Stern Gang"—as ruthless in its headline-seeking prosecution of judges as was the gang seeking the establishment of the State of Israel in the 1940s. Charges were preferred against me accusing me of using my office to aid and assist a friend (Ms. Lancaster). There were strong suggestions that there had been some sexual relationship between me and Ms. Lancaster. This, of course, was grist for the tabloid press and its head-lines that mentioned a "blond model" and the black judge.

These scandalous charges were referred to a retired State Supreme Court justice for a full-fledged hearing, where it became clear that the Stern Gang had nothing of substance to show that I had misused my position to help Ms. Lancaster. The Referee, after an extensive hearing, dismissed almost all of the charges. The Stern Gang, however, persuaded the Commission members to vote to reinstate them all. Once again, after hearing arguments, I was censured. I was represented at the time by the Center For Constitutional Rights. The censure was not without some dissents. Some members wished to banish me from the bench. The majority voted for censure. I understood perfectly. Gerald Stern had been trying for years to have me removed from the bench. After all, he had been an assistant district attorney whose office regarded me as an enemy who willy-nilly ignored the district attorney's recommendations of bail—bail that, from the defendant's point of view, sometimes rivaled the national debt. I had invariably moved to disqualify Gerald Stern as my prosecutor because of his obvious and avid bias and his preconceived notions that simply because charges were preferred, I must be guilty.

That incident marked my last appearance before Stern's notorious Committee. No matter how correct I had been in exercising my judicial discretion in matters of bail and other controversies, my colleagues never spoke out in support. In fact, in one instance, Harold Rothwax, now sitting as an Acting Supreme Court justice, offered his testimony on my behalf, but when I called upon him, he had changed his mind—or had it changed. Criminal Court judges are at the mercy of a mayor for their reappointment and many submit meekly to being "good little judicial children," so as to appease the committees before which those seeking reappointment must appear. Mayor Edward Koch made it clear that, as my ten-year term drew to a close, he would not reappoint me. Apparently, that view has undergone some changes, for he was heard to say on ABC-TV, February, 1996, that he would have reappointed me but was never given the opportunity. He expressed the view that I was a good judge.

My exposure to administrative harassment did not cease after my Criminal Court term was over. However, the two years after I was elected to the Civil Court were so uneventful that they seemed serene by comparison with the first decade of the seventies. For example, I received my mail regularly, something that seldom happened in the Criminal Court. Before creation of the United States Tennis Center in Flushing Meadow, it was my habit to spend a portion of my vacation time at the United States Open Tennis Championships then held at Forest Hills. Each year, I would purchase season tickets. One summer, when controversy and a bad press were raging about my exercise of discretion, and anonymous hate mail was pouring in, my tickets, mailed to me, disappeared somewhere in the Criminal Court before they could reach me. Even today, after more than one year of retirement, some of my mail, sent to the Supreme Court, has been returned to the senders, with the bare-bones endorsement "no longer at this address," although the people at the court know my address very well and I am listed in the Manhattan telephone directory, as I have been for more than fifty-five years. Even the Office of Management Support, of the Unified Court System, as late as 1995 addressed mail to me simply as "Judge Bruce, 72 Thomas St., New York, NY 10013," a rather odd comment on both "Management" and "Support."

While I have witnessed some rather bitter hostility on the part of some judges towards lawyers and defendants, I had never thought of judges being false and unkind to each other. I was naive and apparently, I continue to be. My first exposure was to the aforementioned Judge James S. Watson, one of the city's first black judges. A fastidious and dignified gentleman, he was a true professional. The very term "judge" was awe-inspiring, representing a pinnacle of respected success in the law. It was a title, I thought, that was won on the basis of intellectual and moral merit. It was much later in life, after I became a judge, that I learned what a highly competitive political prize the title and position can be. The usual complications of political favoritism have become even more confused by community interest and its committees created to penetrate the longtime mystery of *who* the judges are. For years, judgeships were regarded as plums to be dispensed by political bosses. Despite the existence of such politics in New York, I believe the state has been lucky in the quality of some of its judges. Some have come to the bench with their ideals intact, despite the political process most must endure. There are still, however, some leftovers from the old days, the "good old days," when political bosses were area dictators, the kinds of bosses that the Seabury Investigation exposed to public scrutiny.

The administrative judge of the Manhattan branch of the state supreme court during my last year on that bench was (and still is) Stanley S. Ostrow. Ostrow appears to be a leftover, a "last hurrah" remnant of the old-time regime of Ed Flynn, formerly the Democratic Party boss of the Bronx. Ostrow's roots are in the Bronx. Not known as a scholar or intellectual, he clearly owes his place on the bench to the power of "Boss Flynn" politics. As my retirement neared in 1995, I spoke to him about working as a judicial hearing officer. Many retired justices and judges assumed such assignments. The pay was $250 per day, a paltry sum when you consider that lawyers appearing before a judicial hearing officer were billing at $250 per hour or more. Ostrow said he had to see that some "good" judges received such work. He had, of course, described me, more than once, as one of the court's hard workers and one who had never refused any request coming from his office. Mistakenly, I assumed from that that I would receive assignments as a JHO. I received one assignment that was first adjourned and then aborted. After several months without an assignment, I investigated and found that the white retired judges were working steadily, although assignments to black retired judges were few and far-between. Disturbed by this, I wrote to Ostrow in April, 1995, telling him that the white retired judges were working "on a fairly steady basis. Is there the same kind of discrimination affecting judicial hearing officers that tainted the system by which acting supreme court justices were appointed?" I asked.

I pointed out to Ostrow that it was rumored that in order to receive steady work, a JHO had to be "buddy-buddy with the appointing authority," and as I had never been, it was perhaps the reason why I had never been an acting supreme court justice when I was a Civil Court judge and, before that, a Criminal Court judge. I then tendered my resignation as a judicial hearing officer, effective immediately. It was well known that administrative judges who affected the appointment of acting supreme court justices virtually controlled them and some of their determinations. Such acting justices, who welcomed the increase in their salaries, were cautious about offending the administrative judge who could cut off the increased income of the acting justice and return him or her to their lower court.

Ostrow's response to my letter of criticism and resignation (in every sense of that term), curiously, was not one of denial or counterclaim. He simply wrote that he was "saddened" by my letter. I, too, was saddened by the necessity of my letter and the harm being done to an old and famous institution, the Supreme Court. I had imagined that my election to the Supreme Court would free me from all of the attacks and controversy that followed me in the lower courts. In those days, I was the target of continuing attacks from Mayor Edward I. Koch. At one point near the end of my term as a Criminal Court judge, Koch asked his committee on judicial appointments to give him a report on me. This, of course, was part of the Koch intimidation tactic, at a time when I would be up for reappointment. Indeed, in the Newfield-DuBrul book, *The Permanent Government: Who Really Runs New York?* the authors write that "Koch had made Wright one of his black punching bags ever since his campaign for mayor in 1977." The book then went on to say that "The *Daily News* had frequently attacked Wright's liberal bail policies, and the police union had compared the jurist to Hitler on more than one occasion. Wright often responded in kind, and was already perceived as a symbol of black extremism by much of white New York."

While I served in the Criminal Court, it was as though Koch was a cheerleader for my defrocking and banishment to his personally selected Coventry. I have no doubt that it was Koch's sniping and bitter name-calling that inspired much of the hate mail that I received during my Criminal Court years. One writer, revealed as a multiple complainer by his handwriting, wrote:

> "Drop dead Bruce Wright, lousy nigger.
> The niggers mug, rob and kill the
> Whites morning, noon and night, And you free them.
>
> Down with the niggers. To hell with them."

Another writer, adding an element of religious miracle to his venom, wrote: "Drop dead nigger. Drop dead twice." Others wrote equally inspirational messages. Some told me that I'd better watch my back and that I would soon be killed, along with my children. Some were signed by those who characterized themselves as police officers. Many were simply irate citizens who quoted Mayor Koch.

As I walked through the streets of Harlem or Brooklyn, people I did not know would yell words of encouragement, urging me to continue to "Tell it like it is!" or "Don't let them get to you; keep up the good work." It was curious to see that the blacks and Hispanics believed I was doing a good job, exactly what a judge should do, while white New York and the tabloid press believed just the opposite. An example of this kind of view is found in the attitude of many prosecutors, for they seem fond of getting rid of potential jurors who are black, if the defendant is black. They seemed fearful that black jurors might ignore the evidence to acquit a black defendant, especially if the complaining witness happened to be white, or a police officer. It was an oblique reminder of Thomas Jefferson's fear that the blacks might one day outnumber the whites in the colonies and seek vengeance for their enslavement.

One of the fascinating and subtle, or not so subtle, aspects of the law is that when a lawyer seeks to have a case tried before a particular judge, because it is felt that the judge is fair and allows counsel to present his or her case, this is derisively characterized as "judge shopping." Yet, whenever a jury cannot reach a unanimous agreement and is "hung," district attorneys have no hesitation about seeking a new trial before a new jury that they hope will see matters as they do.

This, of course, is little more than jury shopping, a tolerated procedure. To some, including me, the new trial is a clear case of double jeopardy, although our highest courts have thus far refused to go that far.

Though in fact I may seem to have favored the criminal side in my capacity, I did not have to be concerned about such matters, for the administrative judges deliberately limited my assignments. I was never allowed to preside over felony trials or criminal trials of any kind. The closest I came to trials touching upon criminal prosecutions was when I was assigned to state mental institutions to listen to psychiatrists and others and then determine whether an accused was insane and should be hospitalized as legally insane and unable to be tried. But even that is a civil proceeding. The court administrators, if they had had their thinking caps on properly, would have assigned me to the persistent felony part of the court where repeat felons are tried and where a judge has little or no discretion and *must* impose heavy prison sentences on those found guilty after trial. That would have shattered my reputation as a judicial liberal.

I never thought of myself as a "liberal," in any event. My efforts on the bench were, I hope, in the tradition of humanism: honor the presumption of innocence and give everyone, accuser and accused, a fair trial, whether on the civil or criminal side. It was always important that lawyers have a full opportunity to present their competing cases, in a courtroom that made counsel comfortable and at ease, so far as the bench could create such an atmosphere, free of judicial oppression and impatience. I have always been mindful of the advice given to me with an understanding smile by Dennis Edwards, a Criminal Court judge for a number of years before I joined him on the bench. He said, "Bruce, there's one thing you must remember when sentencing a defendant and that is, he may be one of your neighbors." Except for some years in my youth, when I lived on West 66th Street and for a short time in Brooklyn, I have lived for over fifty years in Harlem. To this day, I meet people who have been tried in my courtroom, or who have been sentenced by me and it is a comfort to me when they greet me in the street and assure me that I had turned their lives around. It is especially touching when long-ago defendants who expressed their appreciation for some help by saying they were going to name their first child for me. And several have exhibited to me pictures of their daughters, all named "Bruce." As one of the fathers said, "After how you helped me, there's no way I wasn't going to keep my word."

My election to the State Supreme Court gave me a sense of employment comfort and a real sense of having escaped from the controversies, hate mail, threats, and negative publicity of the Criminal Court. I was wrong, of course, for the civil side of the Supreme Court has its traps and surprises as well. No press mention of anything attributed to me failed to mention my police nickname as "Turn 'em Loose Bruce," as though that ancient history was newsworthy. It was while I was serving in the Supreme Court that the Commission on Judicial Conduct made its most persistent and serious effort to have me removed in shame from the bench. It was there, as well, when Stanley Ostrow became administrative judge of the Manhattan branch of the Supreme Court. Then, as well as later, he brought to his chores an unabashed sense of the kind of political bossism that was always inspiring threats of scandalous investigations. Even after I retired, political retaliation was directed at me. He did not like my accusation that racism influenced some of his determinations.

During the 1996 celebration of the birthday of Dr. Martin Luther King, Jr., for example, I was invited by a member of the committee making program arrangements to be the keynote speaker in the Rotunda of the Supreme Court. I welcomed the opportunity and prepared my address. Racism, of course, is not the world's most popular subject. It arouses tension in some and at least temporary embarrassment in others. For me, it is rather like performing exploratory surgery upon myself with a dull scalpel and without the benefit of anesthesia. Or, worse, it is like being the only waiter at a banquet of white cannibals, where the entree is my head upon a platter, and I am condemned to do the carving while the cannibals scream for seconds. However, horrible or not, the racist monster in America must be confronted, lest it devour us all like the neanderthal beast that it is.

It must have been a special prize to Ostrow to have discovered that Lancelot Hewitt, the young court attorney charged with making the King Day arrangements, had invited me to speak. Exercising his power of censorship and suppression, Ostrow ordered that the format of the celebration be changed, I was cancelled and instead of a speech by me, one of the judges presented a small and inoffensive play. I learned this when Hewitt telephoned me (he would put nothing in writing) to say that I had been cancelled. When I saw Hewitt at a New York State Bar Association meeting, I confronted him with accusations that he and his committee had simply caved in in a most shameful manner for lawyers allegedly interested in fair play. While conceding that Ostrow had intervened, he said he had no choice. But he did. He could have easily had a rump session of celebration convened in a hall-way, or even the street to oppose the kind of raw bias exhib-ited by Ostrow. By not doing so, Hewitt and his committee conveyed the impression that they had been cowards in yield-ing without a whimper. Accepting such heavy-handed and crass prior censorship could also be interpreted as conveying a message that the oppressed actually enjoy suppression and the bias that energizes it. Without offering resistance to polit-ical infection poisoning the courthouse we, as lawyers in that workplace, contribute a scandal of our own.

I have had a long and passionate love–hate affair with the law. I remain unforgiving of the so-called Founding Fathers, those pious thieves who took over what has become America, while banishing the Indians to remote ghettos we call reservations. Little wonder that America has been called the greatest example of geographic grand larceny the world has ever see, with the possible exception of the looting of Africa by Europeans. Without continued resistance, from within and from without, our system of justice will make as much sense as a nudists' fashion show of The Emperor's New Clothing. Without consistent and continued opposition to the forces that diminish humane fairness in our system, we will be a straggling group of mute cheerleaders, latter-day searchers for the ideal of Diogenes, or itinerant worshipers wandering among the chaos of fractured ideals. It gives great joy to the bigots who have community satraps like Ostrow in charge of administering justice. It encourages those of meager intellect to believe that, they too, can rise to the height of their incompetence and enjoy before their names the pale-face pre-fix of "Honorable."

While I am grateful for the extraordinary and unexpected

opportunity to have been a judge and to have served my city and state, I continue to believe that judges are selected without proper inquiry into the character of each candidate and that all judges should be civil servants who are subjected to instruction prior to being eligible to ascend the bench. Winning an A+ in the study of corporations, conflict of laws, evidence and estates and trusts, cannot alone assure that academic honors will provide the bench with a humanist.

For many years, I have ridiculed formal religion and especially Christianity. Often, I have wondered about and been baffled by the passionate allegiance of blacks to Christianity, the religion of the slaveowners. And yet the black church, time after time, came to my rescue and support whenever I was caught up in some vexatious controversy. Rev. Herbert Daughtry, of Brooklyn's House of The Lord church, strove mightily in my behalf, staging demonstrations. One Easter, he surrendered his pulpit to me and, in the presence of most of the network cameras, he authorized me to say whatever I wished. And whenever I campaigned for election, Rev. Manny Wilson of the Convent Avenue Baptist Church offered refuge to me and the support of the Baptist Conference of ministers. His church was filled to capacity on one occasion, when he had James Baldwin and Angela Davis there to regale the crowd in my behalf. Wyatt T. Walker's Caanan Baptist Church also offered to advertise my cause and to solicit votes. Rev. Calvin Butts allowed me to debate district attorneys and others and to air my views.

Even so, I feel shriven of a Scarlet Letter by my retirement, despite the burden of years as I near eighty and the brink of the twenty-first century. In retirement, I have never been busier. As a Visiting Professor at the Cooper Union's

School of Architecture, I teach Advanced Concepts and have been permitted to embrace a wide-ranging group of intriguing subjects. The bright young students who pay no tuition at Cooper Union—but who must pass a stern entrance examination—provide me with a transfusion of youth that is sorely needed at my age. I look forward to each class. On October 6th, 1995, as I tooled up Adam Clayton Powell, Jr. Boulevard on my bicycle, at the very moment that I saw a collision with a speeding car was unavoidable, the thought that passed through my head was that I was going to miss a lecture. I barely had time to utter the classic one-syllable word of absolute frustration, "Shit!" before being tossed by the inevitable mismatch of bicycle and car.

I am often invited to make public speeches at universities and law schools and I now do so without being summoned before some commission or authority that demands an explanation of my seasons of discontent. My efforts are now devoted to avoiding the horrors of some mortal affliction, or using the one free gift certificate to become a patient of Dr. Kevorkian. In the meantime, I hope that I can follow the injunction of Dylan Thomas to ". . . not go gentle into that good night, / Old age should burn and rave at close of day;" as I "Rage, rage against the dying of the light."

MORE ABOUT NÉGRITUDE ET MOI

I have written earlier about Léopold Sédar Senghor who played a rather important role in my life, despite the fact that, since my rootless days in Paris immediately after World War II, I have met with him only infrequently. When he was a professor at the Colonial University of France, he was relatively unknown as a poet. After the war, his reputation became international. Essentially a black Frenchman, he loved living in Paris. Indeed, when he was a member of his country's national assembly, Senegal was a member of what was known as The Mali Federation, as though independence was such a strange condition for both Mali and Senegal, that both needed each other in order to survive a new beginning. When that federation fell apart, as though there could be no fruitful sharing of independence, Senghor was called to be the President of Senegal. His first reaction seemed to be one not of jubilation for the greatest honor that a country can confer; even while he was in the National Assembly, he had always preferred to spend six months in Paris and six elsewhere, not always including Senegal.

A very elegant man who spoke perfect and precise French in a way that honored the language, his tenure as president of Senegal was marked by academic festivals and occasional colloquies. Their announced purpose was to venerate and advertise the black genius for culture. As a poet, Senghor wrote stunning tributes to the beauty of black women. And, indeed, his first wife was the daughter of Felix Eboue, the first black governor general of a French colony, although the French preferred the fiction of "overseas" Department and not the demeaning term, colony. His marriage was an event in Paris. While the marriage did produce some children, it did not last.

Senghor was much in demand as a public official and as a poet. This took him away from home for long periods of time. He was also preoccupied with Négritude. Senghor brushes aside such caustic condemnations of the concept as Ezekiel Mphahele's book, *The African Image*. Mphahele asks, "What price Négritude, if the subject is anything other than a revulsion against European society?" Posing another question, he speaks of it as a "spiritual abandonment of a sinking cultural ship"—or so its proponents think. On the other hand, he describes Négritude as dealing in "sheer romanticism" and "mawkishness." He cites Senghor's poem "Prayer Masks" as a purely romantic pose "and an exercise in the rhetoric of his French masters." Mphahele, a South African black, condemns French-speaking black nationalists who claim to reject white culture and nevertheless marry European women.

Mphahele, of course, is subject to the same criticism of miscegenation since he also writes in the language of his colonial conquerors. Still, Senghor maintains his passionate love affair with Negritude and, at the same time, his worship of European culture. Indeed, he is now one of the stewards of French culture as a member of the French Academy. And, despite all of the ridicule directed at him for placing culture before economic development, he remains a highly regarded and affectionate friend of mine. He seems torn by internal urgency, for, on the one hand, he *is* French; on the other, he seems bedazzled by his African blood. I will never forget his contemptuous snort, as he described the wife of one of his cabinet members as a *metisse*. And, when I reminded him of

his son, Paul—his son by his French wife—with equal disdain, he said, *"metisse, aussi!"* Anyway, his poetry is beautifully conceived, even in translation and may be said to have
a genetic energy derived from the best of both bloods.

Although he professed incomplete happiness over the
honor of being called to the presidency of Senegal, Senghor
entered upon his political chores enthusiastically. He moved
into the magnificent building that was the home of the former
French governors-general. Surrounded by well-preened
lawns sloping down to the sea, there were exotic animals and
birds roaming free. Whenever I visited, he put me up in a
three-room suite that looked out over a public park. From the
comfort of my wealthy surroundings, I could see how the
Senegalese lined up each morning to get water from a single
faucet there. In addition to the three men who waited upon
me in their starched uniforms, a chauffeur with a large
Citroen was also assigned to me. The men in my palace quarters would confer each morning to determine what I wished
for lunch and what kind of French wine. I was allowed to
have guests; the two men assigned to me refused to sit and
dine, despite my invitation that they do so.

I was always irked that my passport never got stamped
during my visits and departures from Dakar. Whenever I
arrived, the president always had me met by his chief of pro-
tocol, who whisked me around customs and into a limousine.
I was completely spoiled by such royal attention and I wal-
lowed in it happily, although it was sad to see so much poverty outside the palace. I assumed that whatever wealth I did
see was provided by the French Government. My thoughts of
Senegal were put in a poem I called "My Mother As
Stranger." It memorialized some of my feelings and emotions

during a 1970s colloquy that Senghor fashioned to celebrate
Négritude as it affected every aspect of life:

I was given a suite with a view of the sea;
My terrace was shaded, with a garden below
Where a remarkable bird in a tropical tree
sang out a mystery no mortal could know.
Caretakers of whim were placed at my will
to guarantee whatever I wished when I ate;
fiery flowers on a bright window sill
formed a <u>mise en scene</u> for the highest estate;
It must have been so for Eden's seraphim
or Kubla Khan's sinful Pleasure Dome;
such splendor must have caused Satan some grief,
it was paradise found, entailed with my claim,
yet the vision survives with vague disbelief
like John Donne's three-person'd God.

II

I broke bread in Eden with the sun held at bay;
the delicate china and each sterling device
reflected a Byzantine, long-vanished day;
I thought of those Romans, their casting of dice:
For a moment, the tableau resurrected the dead
and I was a bodyless Baptist regarding my head.

III

The President catered to my gross appetite

as I sat in his palace and enjoyed his board;
it was an urban peasant's exotic delight,
much more fitting for a duchess or lord.
Such pageant and pomp should have led me to weep;
but seduced by manners and silver and gold,
I banished the poor from my visions and sleep.

IV

Independence, I found, keeps old ceremonials
that once dazzled the African colonials;
when Caesar left Gaul to return to Rome,
the vanquished then moved into his home.

V

When I broke bread with the well-dressed Chief,
he seemed quite royal, the king of his fief;
he was President, the host at his table
in surroundings that rivaled a majestic fable:
A giant lobster, polished and dead
had gleaming eyes bulged from its head;
it revealed a taxidermist's flair,
this native menu arranged for our fare.

I was ravished by such an exotic garnish
that put so shame Madame Tussaud's varnish;
the soup, the stroganoff, the salad,
were fit for an ancient sultan's ballad;
a hymn from Michelin, a three-star accolade

should place the chef quite close to God;
I banished subversion and refused to disturb
a banquet that was so delicious, superb.

And in that poor land of black circumstance,
where poor natives seemed to survive by chance,
the dessert was Royal Dame Blanche and
*   fraid du bois:*
I wept internally and mumbled, "Pourquois?"

I could not, of course, show these thoughts to the President, especially during his weeklong symposium, while learned papers celebrated Négritude were being delivered in the language of the colonizers! The concept seemed more ephemeral than ever as defined by the various speakers. Most of the intellectuals present seemed to accept the definition provided by a white man, Jean-Paul Sartre. He decreed that Négritude is a vision, but an able one, of how to be racial without being racist. Since he was a descendant of the colonial invaders of Senegal, some tense delegates wondered how Albert Camus would define Négritude. At least, he was an African, albeit not a black one.

A Nigerian sculptor was fiercely British in a severely tailored suit that could have come from Savile Row. But he did not sweat, despite the equatorial temperature. He bemoaned the fact that there were so few statues of black heroes of African independence, and that those that had been commissioned were by Greek or Italian sculptors. He himself was quite notorious for what he calls his "great master-work," an heroic rendering in Italian marble of Queen Elizabeth II. "I know that bastard," whispered Hoyt Fuller, next to whom I sat. I was not certain whether his epithet was directed at the sculptor or the Queen.

A young and confident speaker from Niger, obviously a poet, spoke in strophes and antistrophes of impressive grace and striking directness. He made bold to question the divine right of Négritude's elder statesmen (including President Senghor, who listened intently.) He added that those of his mood and temper should think in terms of the proper time for cultural coup d'etat, since all all-male concept of Négritude leadership was suspect, in view of the great women poets, such as Gwendolyn Brooks, not to mention other female writers and poets. Observant delegates noticed a fleeting and painful wince cross the face of Senghor at the mention of the word "coup," but he managed a wan and tolerant smile.

During my months of being AWOL after the war, living in Paris, Senghor had been my savior, so to speak, both with food and work at *Présence Africaine*. He was so French. Still, I could utter no word of criticism. He was my friend. Some of his critics, however, did raise questions concerning his acceptance of the French occupation, perhaps even as a collaborationist. After all, his higher education had been taken in France. I admired Senghor's grace and delicacy, no matter how harsh the dialogue became when directed at him. From time to time, he hosted large cocktail parties in the Presidential Palace. One of the guests was a young white woman who was working on her doctoral thesis. She said she was doing an in-depth comparison between Senegal and Cote D'Ivoire. In all candor, she said, Senegal did not come off as well as its neighbor. With exquisite French manners, Senghor chided her gently with the remonstrance that she should remember that Cote D'Ivoire was much richer in natural resources than Senegal.

The colloquy concluded on a sunny April day with a brilliant gala at the Senegalese National Theater. There were some ethnic dances and folklores, somewhat too sweetly choreographed and precise and thus deprived of personal passion. By Senghor's command, it was done in honor of Katherine Dunham. There was also some tribal singing and some sly humor that emerged from the instantaneous interpretation of the Senegalese dialect, Wolof. Just prior to the curtain being raised for a drama celebrating the anti-French heroism of a Wolof warrior, a young American from Washington, DC, saying he represented something called The DC Black Front, (he was tribally splendid in a colorful dashiki and somewhat arranged bouffant Afro hairdo) unleashed a bitter and scornful attack upon his fellow delegates who had declined to join him in his journey into the Medina. Deep in the native quarter, he said, he mixed with the peasants who, he said, were his true brothers and sisters. He excoriated those he described as members of a Black Bourgeoisie pretenders society; he said they were collaborationists (without saying with whom). He said he had nothing in common with them, except skin color. He lauded his self-described status as a "street activist," and he bragged about his ability to eat without a knife or fork.

Many of us marveled at his passion and believed that he was ready to be shriven of his Western manners and apply for Medina citizenship. We were wrong. He was the first one on the plane for his return to Washington. There is no known record of whether, on the long flight, he ate his airline food with or without plates and silver.

Senghor never reproved me, even mildly, for my lack of interest in "returning" to Africa as a homeland. As with other black Americans, I believe it is far too late to try to undo the melancholy diaspora and fly over the Middle Passage to where it all started, that dark tidal wave of humanity that was to give America its troublesome racial dilemma. As though a national taxidermist, America has made its blacks a hodge-podge of irony and paradox, pasting us together in the blood and bones personification of African lookalikes. My Africanist friends do not like this view at all and they consider to refer to Africa as home. But, what country? What village? What tribe? Spoiled and fat on American comforts, I doubt that many of us could tolerate life in an African village, or even a city for that matter. Still, even for me, it is interesting to go to Coney Island and look Eastward towards Africa and Ireland.

After all, with my miscellaneous genes, I must look in different directions for tendrils strong enough to lead to a family tree. I doubt that there are very many blacks in America who can say with any authority that they are one hundred percent black, or African. Still, all of us with a drop of black blood remain curious about our ancestors, both known and unknown. The hope of some, with their curiosity about the past, is that they will learn something significant about themselves. They may not, however, find it in Africa. There were and are, after all, so many tribes that until fairly recently have only had oral traditions, not those preserved in writing.

Despite my affection and esteem for Senghor, I think he was wrong to emphasize culture before advancing economics if he wished Senegal to emerge from the third world. But

Senegal has had stable governments ever since independence, with none of the dictatorial abuse of human rights that is so alarming in Nigeria and the military cruelties that have made Liberia Africa's Yugoslavia.

In a recent letter, Senghor says he no longer writes poetry. He spends time in his Place de Tocqueville apartment in Paris and in his wife's chateau near Caen.

In 1956, he wrote that he wished to have my poetry published in a bilingual edition. He asked Professor Louis Achille, of Lyon, to do the translations. I spent two weeks with Achille one spring, as he consulted at least eight different dictionaries, wrestling with my word arrangements. Ultimately, he gave up, telling Senghor that he could not capture my true flavor in translation. I was disappointed because Achille had been a professor at Howard University and I believed—and still believe—professors are capable of anything. Other more important concerns arose to challenge Senghor's time. The publishing project never occurred.

Sometime later, when Horace M. Bond, the then president of Lincoln University, was visiting Senghor during the Congress of Black Writers, Scholars, and Artists in Paris, he had lunch with Senghor. As he chatted, he talked about the differences in accent and tone of various languages, and the difficulty, in poetry, of creating a common interlanguage music. He said, in a letter to me, that:

> "Senghor suddenly jumped up and said, 'I know *one* master of this art; it is the American, Bruce Wright!'—and he dashed into his study, to bring back a heavily underscored copy of *From The Shaken Tower*. And then he expatiated on the marvelous qualities of your verse, and the joy he took in correspondence with you!

> "Believe me, that was quite the finest impression of

Lincoln University I have ever had!"

It was a great morale booster for me. My sons, however, have never, to my knowledge, read any of my poetry.

AFTERWORD

The term "Afterword" seems so doleful, as though anxious heirs are clustered to hear the reading of a spendthrift's Last Will; but I have a feeling that life ends exactly the way these recollections have concluded, in the middle of a syllable. I have had a wild and passionate love–hate affair with the law and with America. I have remained bitter about America segregating its forces racially to be sent off on some mission of democracy. I remain alarmed by what fate lurks in the future for my children. I counsel them to be happy and do the things that make them so while not neglecting to taste life to the full.

My life has been full of excitement and more joy than sorrow. I have every confidence that, because of my color, I have had many more sociological surprises and experiences than any white man could ever have had. Thus, the episodes of my life have been rather like the Saturday afternoon movies the young used to attend, where one serial would be adjourned to the next, leaving a hero hanging by his fingernails to a sheer cliff, as he remained until the next Saturday to survive for his next death-defying caper.

The women I have loved and who have said they loved me have all been dismayed by my incurable fault of refusing to mature and grow up, by my seeming addiction to puns and the ambiguities of the English language. I suppose, had I been dull and serious, I could have been a success in life, that is, comfortably affluent, with all of the "things" that Socrates sneered at as he walked one day through the Athens agora of his time. And, as usual, as I watched the reactions of people winning lottery millions, I knew that I was better qualified than they to spend such winnings properly and improperly.

Affluent or not, I have savored life, tasting its surprises and sadness as a twentieth-century Everyman. I have been on the fringes of my social betters, ridiculing their well-dressed promenades and imitations of life. I have remained in awe of The Great and, despite my fifty years or more of friendship with Léopold Sédar Senghor, after he became president of his country, I could never address him as "Sédar," the affectionate name he was called by his intimates. When I became a judge, I was in awe of those who already were. Never a hail-fellow well met, after twenty-five years as a judge, there are only three judges that I could address by their first names. I believed for a long time that those ambitious enough to wish to sit as judges were humanists, moved by the most ideal of instincts. I was to learn otherwise as I observed my colleagues doing their brand of justice, conduct that was not often a morality play.

Against my better judgment, I once sat before the governor's committee that recommended to him those judges thought to be worthy of promotion to the Appellate Division of the State Supreme Court. The first question put to me by a professor at the John Jay College of Criminal Justice was, "What makes you think you are qualified to sit among a collegial group of judges?" She then suggested that I was too standoffish, a loner, a constant dissenter, who, ignoring the effect of what he said, expressed his opinions brutally and against the current.

She amused me. After all, there could be no law unless there was controversy to make it necessary. The "System," as we call it, especially that branch known as the judiciary, mandates that freedom of speech must stop at the courthouse door, for judges who wish to kiss the hem of the garment (and higher) of those who have the power to make the gift of promotions. Of course, I understand ambition and how it can drive or stall one along the way of one's career. After all, no one wishes to languish in a dead-end job. Ambition aside, I had always believed that judging was a scholarly calling. Now, I believe it should be. But the scholars are all too often the judicial clerks who draft opinions for the judges and do the burdensome research. I have been the beneficiary of an excellent court attorney (as the judicial clerks are called). Most of "my" decisions that have been found worthy by New York's highest appellate court were the work of my clerk and friend, Debbie Woll. She and I had an unspoken competition in writing opinions that would withstand the highly critical scrutiny of the appellate courts. Debbie made the sometimes drudgery of research and writing worthwhile. She was also a willing ear whenever we shared judicial gossip and rumors.

As I neared the end of my career as a judge, it occurred to me that I had really had an eventful life with many simple things being cherished as important. I believed that my poetry was worthy of publication and I had brief flirtations with publication from time to time. Senghor had expressed his intention to have my poetry published in a bilingual edition. But Louis Achille, to whom he assigned the job of translation, said he could not grasp my idiom. William Rose Benet said I had "promise." Langston Hughes, in a 1948 letter to Arna Bontemps, said he had read some of my poems and liked one "very much," adding, "I think the guy is going places and will surely have another book soon."

That prediction of "soon" came thirty-two years later,

when Dr. Joseph Okpaku, a Nigerian and head of the Third Press International, published a selection of some of my poems. I was grateful and rejoiced when he reported that, except for the copies he gave me, *Repetitions* had sold out.

I never expected to become a judge and had no ambition to be one. I loved the practice of law and to this day, I admire those lawyers who have done only that. I believe that many black lawyers who accept appointment or election to the bench simply believe they can make a more comfortable living that way, with a predictable income. After the hazard of uncertainty that occurred in my life, after my two partners both died in 1966, barely in their thirties, I confess that that is when I yielded to long-standing invitations to become a public servant. My ambition has always been to a poet and to be published. I believe, also, that the title "professor" is the most honorable of callings. And while I have taught at various universities, my greatest delight has been as a visiting professor at the Cooper Union For the Advancement of Science and Art. For that honor, I remain grateful to John Hejduk, dean of the Irwin S. Chanin School of Architecture of Cooper Union. It is he, a poet in his own right and a distinguished architect, who allowed me to read poetry in the Great Hall of Cooper Union and to enjoy the bright young students there.

At seventy-eight, I remain distressingly immature to those who know me best and delightfully so to myself. While I am resigned to racism being America's incurable national disease, I am not immune to its poisons. My fears may be found in a few lines of verse that I wrote when two of my sons were spirited off to Africa by their mother for six years:

Malicious mountains may swallow them all
as they harken to some evil Pied Piper's call;
and then, London Bridge will be ashes in a pile;
Humpty-Dumpty will lie scrambled in his fall;
cuckoos will weep without a clock to call;
Mother Hubbard will wear Medusa's reptile wigs;
Red Riding Hood will rape the wolf in
  grandmother's bed;
The House that Jack built will have tigers
  on its stairs,
and Christmas?
Christmas will be Simple Simon pissing on your head.

—Bruce McM. Wright
Harlem, 1996.

INDEX

DATE			